Kids Out of Control

by
Alan M. Cohen, M.D.

T·H·E

PRESS

19 Prospect Street
Summit, NJ 07901

This book is not intended to replace personal medical care and supervision; there is no substitute for the experience and information that your doctor can provide. Rather, it is our hope that this book will provide additional information to help people understand the complex issues of conduct disorders.

Proper medical care should always be tailored to the individual patient. If you read something in this book that seems to conflict with your doctor's instructions, contact your doctor. Your doctor may have medically sound reasons for recommending treatment that may differ from the information presented in this book.

If you have any questions about any treatment in this book, consult your doctor.

In addition, the patient names and cases used in this book do not represent actual people, but are composite cases drawn from several sources.

Facts About Laurel Oaks Hospital

Laurel Oaks Hospital is an 80-bed psychiatric hospital dedicated to helping children and adolescents who suffer from a wide range of emotional illnesses and problems related to substance abuse. It is one of 60 psychiatric hospitals owned and operated by Psychiatric Institutes of America, part of the NME Specialty Hospital Group.

Contents

DEDICATION

For my parents

AND WITH APPRECIATION

To my patients and their families; whose openness has helped us all to grow.

To the staff of *Operation Redirect*; who rarely receive the recognition they deserve.

To Libby Coker and Larry Hoening; more than assistants, trusted friends.

To James, Richard, Samantha, Carolyn, Stephanie, and Zachary; my children and teachers.

Mostly to Rosemary—she knows why.

And with thanks to Dawn Micklethwaite Peterson for her valuable contributions to this book.

Introduction

Hope in a Hopeless Situation

Peter* was a kid who just couldn't seem to stay out of trouble. When he was only three he was caught throwing rocks at passing cars. Even then his aim was good; twice his parents had to replace broken windshields. By second grade he was known as a troublemaker at school, and by sixth grade his teachers were relieved to send him on to junior high.

Peter began sneaking out of the house at night when he was 12. Later, when he learned to drive, he would steal his mother's car keys and cruise the highways, radio blasting, until dawn. He'd go home in the early morning and fall into bed for a few hours until his mother forced him to go to school. Friendless and flunking out, Peter decided to leave town. All he needed was some cash. A few purse snatchings would do the trick. But he hadn't counted on the off-duty cop. . . .

---

*All names and identifying characteristics have been changed to protect patients' privacy.

KIDS OUT OF CONTROL

Leslie didn't like rules. "Pick up your clothes." "Get to school." "Watch your brother." She'd had it. One day when she was 15 she tossed a few things into a paper bag and moved in with a friend who had her own apartment and a lot of friends who kept the refrigerator full of wine. No more school, no more rules. Leslie spent her days sitting on the floor of the empty apartment, drinking, smoking marijuana, and listening to music. A seemingly endless parade of men floated in and out. Sex was no big deal, just something to do in between getting stoned and drunk. Then her friend told her to get lost. Leslie stole a sleeping bag and moved into the woods. Things weren't too bad until the first frost. . . .

School counselors are very familiar with the syndrome. A child hits adolescence and suddenly runs into problems. Perhaps the boy was always prone to tussles on the grade school playground. Perhaps the girl was always a reluctant scholar. But now these kids are getting into serious mischief: truancy, stealing, drinking, drug use. They're chronically in trouble with teachers and classmates, and they may even have run-ins with the police. No one knows what to do with them. They seem to be their own worst enemies.

"Bad" kids are nothing new. In the 1920s, author August Aichhorn wrote in his now classic book, *Wayward Youth*, about a group of "bad" boys whose misdeed was stealing cherries from a neighbor's orchard.

Quaint by today's standards, this anecdote nevertheless shows that troubled and troublesome young people are not a new phenomenon. Of course, today's problem youth aren't likely to indulge in the fruit-pilfering escapades that tempted their 1920s counterparts. If they steal, the bounty is more likely to be a watch from a classmate's locker, a stereo from a neighbor's house, or perhaps even a car.

THE KIDS NOBODY LIKES

A bad seed. Juvenile delinquent. Hoodlum. Sociopath. Punk. These are all terms used to describe the kid who can't stay out of trouble and often doesn't seem to want to; the kid who is no stranger to court and who may know from firsthand experience what the inside of a jail looks like.

In psychiatry we have another term to describe these kids. By definition, a child who has a persistent pattern of violating the basic rights of others and defying major age-appropriate norms or rules is a child with a **conduct disorder.**

So what's a conduct disorder? The official definition includes thirteen criteria. If the disturbance of conduct lasts at least six months, the presence of any three of the following criteria suggest the diagnosis:

1. Stealing or forging more than once, without confronting the victim.
2. Running away from home overnight at least twice (or once without returning).
3. Lying often (for reasons other than avoiding physical or sexual abuse).
4. Setting fires deliberately.
5. Being truant from school or absent from work frequently.
6. Breaking into a house, building, or car.
7. Destroying someone else's property (other than by setting a fire).
8. Being physically cruel to animals.
9. Forcing someone into sexual activity.
10. Using a weapon in a fight more than once.
11. Starting physical fights often.
12. Stealing by confronting the victim (mugging, purse-snatching, extortion, armed robbery).
13. Being physically cruel to people.

KIDS OUT OF CONTROL

Conduct disorder can be classified as mild, moderate, or severe, depending on how much the undesirable behavior harms others.

Youngsters with conduct disorder are usually the kids nobody likes. Most psychiatrists and therapists go out of their way to avoid treating them. It's true that these young people can be trying to work with. Many of them are highly intelligent, creative, and cunning, and most are smart alecks— threatening, challenging, and aggressive.

But these are the kids I treat at Laurel Oaks Hospital. And what's more, I like them!

I don't know what this says about me as a psychiatrist, but I truly enjoy working with conduct-disordered kids. And I don't believe they're just bad kids incapable of ever being good. Rather, the kids I treat have severe emotional problems for a variety of reasons that we'll explore later. They show extremely bad judgment. Most haven't had adequate supervision. Most haven't learned to control their impulses. Many of them are using unacceptable behavior to act out the conflicts they feel inside.

If you are reading this book, there is a good chance you or someone you know has a child who has behavior problems. It's been hard on the entire family. You may feel powerless and out of control yourself. And you may have lost any hope that this child will ever grow up to be a functioning, productive adult.

There are no guarantees when it comes to treating a kid with a conduct disorder. Many programs seem to work for a while. Then the kid "graduates," goes back home, and resumes his or her old ways.

But I believe a happier scenario can emerge from treatment. After several years of working with conduct-disordered kids, I've developed a program that combines several approaches to changing the way these kids relate to the world. Even though the program is still relatively new, the outcome thus far has been promising.

GETTING THE SITUATION UNDER CONTROL

- If a child has behavioral difficulties, how can you tell if the root cause is just a difficult adolescence or if there are more deeply ingrained, resistant, serious problems?
- What children—because of socioeconomic background, broken homes, parental alcoholism, and other factors— are at high risk for developing conduct disorder?

Reading through the book, you will learn to identify traits in a child, or even an infant, that may predict later conduct problems. You will learn parenting techniques that tend to work well with problem children and that may avert difficulties in adolescence, if applied early enough.

If the bud has already bloomed into a big problem, I will guide you through what, after much trial and error, appears to my mind to be the most successful treatment.

The purpose of this book is to help you help your troubled child. In the short term, I hope it can help you address concrete behavior problems. In the long term, I hope it will steer you in the direction of treatment, which must involve not only the child but the rest of the family as well. The road from teenage delinquency need not necessarily lead to the penitentiary or to general failure in life. As a parent, you are not powerless. You *can* influence the future. But first you need to understand the problem, rather than merely react to the symptoms.

Isn't it worth a try?

PART I

Understanding Conduct Disorders

Chapter 1

"My Kid Is Out of Control"

Larry's mother used to say he started stealing before he was out of diapers. Every time she took him to the grocery store he'd come home with a couple of packs of gum that she hadn't bought. Of course, two-year-olds don't steal. But by the time Larry was halfway through grade school he was adept at stealing other kids' lunch money. His parents were embarrassed by his fast fingers, but they didn't really take the problem very seriously. No one could blame him for taking something he *found*. That wasn't really stealing, was it? When Larry was 14 he was arrested for breaking into a house. It turned out he was responsible for eight burglaries in their small town. In lieu of juvenile detention, Larry was sentenced to treatment in my program for conduct-disordered kids.

As I explained the program to his parents they sat in front of me shaking their heads, dazed, as though they both believed they were in the middle of a nightmare from which they were about to awaken. "But he's such a smart boy," his mother kept saying. "Is it possible the police made a mistake?"

Larry was a charmer, all right. Lots of con men are. The easiest way for his parents to deal with him was to pretend everything was fine. So that's what they did—until events forced them to recognize that their son was out of control.

What is out-of-control behavior? I often hear that question, particularly from parents who are worried that their difficult teenager's rite of passage is stormier than it should be. Usually what they're worried about turns out to be normal adolescent rebellion, which is a pain to live through and to live with, but generally a natural—*and essential*—part of growing up.

However, for an estimated 4 to 20 percent of adolescents— the percentage varies depending on which criteria are used— the problem goes much deeper. These children have varying types and degrees of conduct disorder, which today is one of the most common psychiatric problems in adolescents.

In the current *Diagnostic and Statistical Manual of Mental Disorders*, Revised Third Edition—a sort of "cookbook" approach to psychiatric diagnosis—conduct disorder is defined as the presence of a repetitive and persistent pattern of conduct, for at least six months, in which the basic rights of others are violated.

Conduct disorder has sometimes been further broken down into subcategories: socialized or nonsocialized, aggressive or nonaggressive. According to this system of classification, socialized conduct-disordered kids get along well with people, but only to use and manipulate them. Kids with nonsocialized conduct disorder are loners who have failed to establish normal relationships with others. Those classified as aggressive are often involved in acts of violence, while those called nonaggressive stay away from violence but are at odds with societal norms; they show this through lying, skipping school often, abusing drugs and alcohol, running away from home, vandalizing property, or setting fires.

While these categorizations are helpful, they have their limitations. For example, I could line up six members of a gang, all of whom meet the criteria for conduct disorder. But while their behavior might be identical, the cause or root of that behavior might be different for each one. Thus, treatment would have to be specifically designed for each individual.

Many people assume that any kid with conduct disorder is by definition antisocial—someone who *intellectually* knows the difference between right and wrong, but on an emotional level couldn't care less. These are the true con men types, or worse, the people who commit horrendous crimes and have no pangs of conscience. The old word for them was "psychopaths."

In fact, however, the majority of kids with conduct disorder are not truly antisocial. It's my belief that their objectionable behavior is the result of depression, family stress, learning disabilities, or other problems.

Let's meet both a "nonsocialized" and a "socialized" kid with conduct disorder so we can compare some of their characteristics.

AT WAR WITH THE WORLD

Jeff, 14, a handsome boy with a voice that still retains its youthful squeak, is at war with the world and everything in it. Even in the womb little Jeff kicked so hard and moved so much his mother thought she was surely pregnant with twins. As a baby he walked early and acted like a perpetual motion machine. Keeping up with him was so exhausting that a few of his teenage babysitters refused to come back a second time. At the age of 5, Jeff went into the family garage with a screwdriver and completely disassembled a lawnmower within half an hour. In grade school he was constantly in trouble with his teachers for not paying attention, destroying school property, distracting other children, and starting playground fights.

His parents struggled with him. They set limits, explained the rules, and made sure he understood what was expected. But Jeff went ahead and wreaked havoc anyway, and his parents found themselves caught in a vicious circle of threats and punishments.

They kept hoping he would outgrow the misbehavior and start acting more reasonably. But once Jeff went to junior high, he added beer and drugs to his list of hobbies, and his problem behavior worsened considerably. Now in high school, Jeff has accumulated a long record of misdeeds: assault on teachers; threats to the school principal; tripping the school fire alarm; setting off firecrackers, in a state where even sparklers are illegal; driving under the influence and without a license.

Regrets? Not really. Jeff sometimes acts superficially remorseful. But at other times he boasts of his accomplishments. He likes to tell people what a big man he is in his neighborhood.

Jeff is a junior criminal and a definite threat to society. Without radical intervention he will almost certainly end up behind bars. He knows right from wrong, but he does what he pleases and lets the chips fall where they may. He's more concerned with getting caught and with consequences than with right and wrong. His behavior may be fueled by an attention deficit disorder and by the rejection he experienced as a child. That doesn't change the fact that he's a deeply disturbed kid.

DON'T TOUCH ME

Even as a baby, Sam was a loner. He didn't like to be touched, and he screamed his head off when his mother picked him up. In nursery school he ignored the other kids and played by himself in a corner of the room.

Everyone has seen a Sam. He's the kid nobody ever got to know, the one who just took up space behind a desk in a classroom with twenty-five other desks. He didn't make friends, he didn't share, he didn't respond in class. Sam stayed locked inside himself, as if in an invisible cage. By the time he was 12, he was spending much of the day stoned. But to maintain his constant high he needed money, and that meant stealing from his parents. He rarely went to school, preferring to spend his days lounging in the basement after his parents left for work. When they discovered his truancy, he ran away for four months and lived on the street.

Unlike Jeff, Sam is not an immediate threat to society. He isn't violent. Even as a little boy he was likely to be the victim rather than the aggressor. But Sam is headed down a path of self-destruction. Without successful treatment, Sam, like thousands of others, is destined to live on the fringes of society.

Sam, with his undersocialized, nonaggressive behavior, is less likely to receive treatment than a youth with an aggressive form of conduct disorder. The main reason is that it's aggressive behavior that gets kids in trouble with the law.

THE EARLY SIGNS

A conduct disorder does not spontaneously erupt at the first sign of puberty. Generally, these adolescents have shown some degree of problem behavior and troubled family relations throughout their lives. In a few cases, the early seeds of a later conduct disorder begin to sprout during infancy, with behavior such as extraordinary squirminess, overactivity, difficulty settling into a pattern of sleeping and eating, resistance to small changes such as leaving the sandbox, and throwing unusually long tantrums.

Parents of conduct-disordered children frequently cite such characteristics when they reminisce about their child's babyhood. The trouble is, this kind of reporting may say as much about the parents' level of tolerance as it does about the child's personality. And of course, not every difficult baby grows into a problem child.

However, more specifics emerge as the conduct-disordered child grows. In one study of problem preteen children, the vast majority of parents complained that their child was disobedient. Other problem behaviors mentioned included yelling, fighting, teasing, crying, whining, lying, stealing, and setting fires. All of these may be normal in limited amounts. But if the frequency of such behavior increases, and if the child resists changing even when given clear guidance, a problem may be developing.

Preteen children who are diagnosed as having conduct disorder often steal items that they already have or could get legitimately. One of my current patients, a boy from a well-to-do family, has a history of swiping supplies from the art room at his school.

Although many conduct-disordered kids have above-average intelligence, they tend to do poorly in school. They may have a habit of wandering away from home without asking permission. These children have few friends, and they tend to be in constant conflict with family members and teachers. When caught doing something wrong, they may not appear guilty or show any remorse.

Conduct-disordered children are preoccupied with short-term gains: instant gratification and to hell with the consequences. Like a 2-year-old who wants something and wants it now, the child with a conduct disorder has not learned that waiting can often enhance the payoff.

Does your child have friends? Is he or she invited to other children's homes to play? If your child is conduct-disordered, there is a good chance the answer is no. These children tend to lack social skills. They may be toilet-trained later than other children, often have a difficult time getting along with peers, don't participate well in sports, and do poorly in school.

When it comes to relating to others, the aggressive conduct-disordered child, no matter what his or her age, is very much like the 2-year-old in the sandbox who discovers that the fastest way to get the shovel away from the kid next to him is to grab it. In time, the normal toddler matures and learns social skills that are more effective in the long run than force.

But the kid with aggressive conduct disorder continues to rely on early bully-like behavior to get what he wants. As he grows, so does his repertoire of force.

HOW AGGRESSIVE IS YOUR CHILD?

We all know kids who look like they're fated to end up with their picture on the wall of the Post Office. And then something happens. Ten, fifteen years later, they're graduating from medical school, or teaching American history, or busting criminals in the old neighborhood. Every so often, the block bully turns into a pussycat.

Frequently, however, the bully just gets bigger and stronger. Kids who show abnormally aggressive behavior are more likely to become heavy drinkers during adolescence and alcoholics as adults. At the same time, aggressiveness is associated with delinquency and criminal behavior.

Other factors associated with criminal or antisocial behavior that continues into adulthood include drug use, drinking, truancy, inappropriate sexual activity, going with a bad crowd, being forced to leave home, getting arrested—all before the age of 15.

Do any of these characteristics describe your son or daughter?

Ignores directions
Resistant to discipline
Oppositional
Stays out late
Fights with peers
Physically aggressive toward adults
Overly competitive
Verbally abusive to adults
Involved in vandalism
Sets fires
Vengeful
Cruel to animals or children

Destructive
Repeats troublesome problematic behavior despite
  confrontation and discipline

The more of these symptoms your son or daughter has, the greater the likelihood that the objectionable behavior will persist.

NOT A "COOKBOOK" APPROACH

Diagnosing a conduct disorder is not like reading from a dictionary. Every child is different. Some kids whose behavior is outrageous may not have a conduct disorder, but rather an illness such as schizophrenia. I see a lot of kids with conduct disorders combined with other psychiatric conditions, such as manic-depression and attention deficit disorder (see Chapter 4). Some kids just run with a bad crowd or have to cope with terrible family situations.

As a rule, the child with a conduct disorder:

- Has an extreme reaction to the pressure of separating from the family (pulling away from the family is considered a normal part of growing up); or
- Has had little support from his or her parents, or
- Has chronic low self-esteem; or
- Is bioneurologically predisposed to show abnormal responses to stress.

Although I don't want to dwell here on the importance of environment (see Chapter 3), I want to at least mention the role of the family in conduct disorder. In the vast majority of cases, kids with conduct disorder have a severe character deficit *plus* a family that is not functioning as a cohesive unit.

In short, I rarely see kids with conduct disorders who come from stable homes. And though their parents surely love them, the kids frequently don't *feel* loved.

Lisa, like many kids I see, comes from the kind of home you don't see portrayed on television sitcoms. Her mother had to be hospitalized five times after Lisa's father beat her. When Lisa was in first grade, her father started sexually molesting her. By the time she was 10, she had learned that her home—where one of her four little brothers and sisters was always screaming and her father was always drinking—was a good place to stay away from. Lisa started running with a crowd of older girls who liked to stay out all night drinking and doing drugs. On one of the rare nights she was home, her father raped her. She swore to herself it would be the last time. She stole her mother's diamond ring and the family car. Two days later she was found after she'd wrecked the car. At our first interview she told me all she wanted was a sharp knife so she could kill her father.

WHEN IS BEING "BAD" NORMAL?

A young woman watches in bewilderment as her 2-year-old daughter kicks and screams, banging her head against the wall in a fit of temper because she's been told she can't have a cookie. Uneasy, she asks herself, What's wrong with my child?

The mother of a 14-year-old complains that she and her daughter used to be such good friends; now they can barely speak without a volcano of accusations and bad feelings erupting.

A father fears that his once straight-A son may be taking drugs because the boy's grades have dropped.

A boy is caught driving under the influence. A high school girl begins lying and staying out late.

You wonder what's wrong with your child. Is he or she turning into a "bad" kid?

In most cases, the answer to that question is no.

The 2-year-old who never has temper tantrums or who is reluctant to yank a toy away from a playmate is more cause for concern than one who does. Being negative is a big part of being a toddler. The 2-year-old is struggling between being his own person and running to Mommy every time the urge hits.

In many ways, an adolescent is like a toddler. Torn between wanting the safety of Mommy and Daddy's arms and the freedom and excitement of the vast world, the teenager is understandably ambivalent. The task of adolescence is to separate from the family of one's birth and eventually move into the family of one's choice. This separation process can be traumatic for everyone involved. You say black, your teenager says white.

No one ever said being a parent—especially the parent of an adolescent—is easy. But with a little patience, a sense of humor, and a good memory of what adolescence was like for you, it may turn out that you actually enjoy the process known as adolescence.

To better evaluate the behavior of a child who is out of control in an abnormal sense, let's first explore the boundaries of "normal" teenage behavior.

Chapter 2

What Is A Normal Teenager, Anyway?

No matter how old we get, most of us can recall an event in adolescence that left an indelible mark.

Did you ever have a date with the captain of the football team or the head cheerleader, only to have your long-awaited dream turn into a nightmare? You woke up the morning of the big day with a face full of pimples. You found out too late that your mother sent your best outfit to the cleaners. You spilled soup on yourself at dinner, and during the movie you were sweating so badly, you were terrified your deodorant wasn't doing its job. In fact, you were so nervous that you couldn't think of anything halfway amusing or intelligent to say. So you smiled a lot and said little. And the next day you heard through the grapevine that as a date, you were a big zero.

"These are the best years of your life." Most of us probably heard that from our parents when we were adolescents. Perhaps they had forgotten the negative and only remembered the positive—forgot what it was like to search for a comfortable identity and to have so much of that identity, as fragile as an eggshell, hinge on the opinions of others. Maybe they just remembered the freedom. While they were working all day to feed and clothe us, we were worrying about our grade in English, whether we would be chosen for the basketball team, or if someone would ask us out on Saturday night. To them, these worries were hardly earth-shattering.

It is true that for some lucky kids, adolescence is a happy time. These teens are like sturdy vessels in perennially calm waters. For some reason—often because of good looks, athletic prowess, or leadership abilities—they breeze through these years without major conflict. This doesn't mean that there's no inner struggle. Nor does it mean life will always be so easy; usually it won't be. But for some reason, these kids have what it takes to be "wildly successful" teenagers.

In the middle are the average kids. Recent studies indicate that contrary to common belief, most adolescents are not in constant turmoil and angst. They're eager to become individuals, and at the same time eager to fit into the peer culture. They may have many episodes of self-doubt, insecurity, and embarrassment, but the problems are mostly short-lived. They win a few, lose a few, and try to roll with the punches.

At the far end of the spectrum is the adolescent who's miserable. Anna was such a girl. "Dr. Cohen," she said between sobs, "if these are the best years of my life, I might as well kill myself now."

Twenty pounds overweight, Anna was extremely intelligent but made only average grades. She was depressed and unable to concentrate on her studies. Moreover, she had few friends, and even though she was in her junior year in high school, she had never had a date. Painfully shy, Anna felt as though she—and all her faults—were constantly on display. She compared herself to a specimen on a slide with her peers behind the microscope, carefully examining her frailties.

A lot of teenagers find adolescence a chore rather than a challenge. Some, like Anna, are perfectly miserable. Others find their teen years a bittersweet time, a mixed blessing of conflicts resolved and rewards gained: a time of identity consolidation.

CHANGING BODIES, CHANGING MINDS

It seemed to her mother that practically overnight Stacey had changed—from the tomboy who wouldn't even stand still long enough to have her hair combed, to the prima donna who liked nothing better than to gaze at herself in the mirror, trying out different hairstyles and shades of lipstick.

At 12, Stacey was starting to mature. Her formerly boyish figure was developing the curves of womanhood. She started menstruating. Boys, formerly beneath her notice, now interested her immensely. She seemed unable to stop giggling when a guy was around. Her mother called her boy-crazy.

During adolescence something inside our bodies clicks, the result being a surge of the hormones that turn girls into women and boys into men. These hormones are not only responsible for your daughter's burgeoning breasts and your son's squeaky voice; they also translate into enormous energy, more energy than your child will ever have again. Have you ever wondered how it is that your teenager can sustain his or her constant motion? By ten o'clock you're ready to turn out the light, but your 16-year-old could dance until dawn and still have enough energy to wolf down a gigantic breakfast with gusto. Blame it on this sudden surge of hormones—don't you wish it could be bottled?

One minute Jake was on a natural high, in love with the world and everything in it; the next, he was shoving his sister away from the TV set or sulking in his room behind a locked door.

Let's face it: Teenagers behave erratically. Some days it may seem that everything is all black, some days all white. As adults, we've gained some perspective. We know that if something bad or annoying happens one day, well, no big deal; there's always tomorrow. Teenagers live more in the here and now. They have yet to learn the patience of age and the necessity for compromise. To the teenager, every emotion, every action seems to be held under a magnifying glass. That's why the tiniest slight—a terse word from a friend, a rebuke from a teacher, a near miss for a spot on the cheer-leading squad—can seem like the end of the world.

FREEDOM—OF A SORT

It seemed only yesterday that Linda still held her mother's hand when they crossed the street. Then, as if by magic, the little girl became an adolescent and the rules changed. The child who had once sought the reassuring touch of her mother's hand now avoided even being *seen* with a parent.

The teenage years are most kids' first taste of freedom. Suddenly they're allowed to "cross the street" without an adult. Friends and activities with friends take priority over family relationships. Ask your teenager if he or she wants to go shopping with you, and you're apt to get an unenthusiastic response. But that same kid will jump at a friend's suggestion that they go to the mall.

The freedom to spend the day with friends. The freedom to drive a car. The freedom to date. All this freedom can be intoxicating for the kid who not so long ago was used to having his mother pick out his socks for him. Suddenly he's expected to pick out his own socks and much more: Away from the prying eyes of adult authority, he can decide whether he's going to smoke, drink, take drugs, and have sex. This was a kid whose biggest decisions not so long ago were which cartoons to watch on Saturday morning and whether to have cake or pie for dessert.

YOU AGAINST ME

Louis enjoyed a warm relationship with his family. For as long as he could remember, the family had done everything together. In the winter they skied. In the summer they went camping. Weekends were devoted to family outings. Most nights the family ate together, with everyone gathered together around the big oak table sharing the best—and worst—parts of their respective days.

Then everything changed when Louis turned 14. He seemed to drift away from the family setting, preferring to spend hours in his room, headphones blasting. His parents no longer could interest him in weekend football games or movies. And dinnertime became a test of everyone's endurance. One night a sullen Louis would pick at his food without saying a word; the next he would launch into a diatribe against the family's upper-middle-class lifestyle.

At some point in our emotional and physical development, we must begin to separate from our family. Successful adolescence depends on a family unit that can tolerate and encourage separation, but at the same time provide a safety net in times of trouble.

Essentially, this means allowing your teenager breathing room, while at the same time letting him or her know that you're still available in times of trouble. The adolescent wants to begin making personal decisions, and some of those decisions will not be the right ones. So often I see parents wringing their hands over their teenagers. "She's making a big mistake," a father insists, shaking his head. "Why won't he listen to us?" another parent asks.

In a perfect world, the young might be able to fully benefit from the experience of their elders. We could say to our children, "Believe us. We know more than you. We've traveled that road and we know that at this junction it's better to turn right, not left." In the real world, though, young people must make their own mistakes, at least some of the time. That's how they learn, and the process itself is valuable. It's worth the price of a few mistakes.

As parents we can offer our opinions. We can provide guidance and set limits for acceptable behavior. And we can be there to cushion the sometimes inevitable fall. But we cannot keep our children from growing away from us.

NO LONGER MOMMY'S LITTLE GIRL

If not for you, she wouldn't be here. You carried her inside you for nine months and went through immense pain bringing her into the world. You nursed her at your breast and wiped her bottom. You took loving care of her through the usual childhood illnesses and cuddled her when she had bad dreams.

Our children are so important to us, and such a part of us, that it can be easy to forget that they are separate beings. We don't own them. For many years we take it upon ourselves to govern their lives because they are too young to take charge. Then, little by little, they begin taking over that role. They tell you—sometimes in many words, sometimes more subtly—to butt out. They demand their privacy. They don't always want us around, and that hurts.

Eileen tacked a large sign to her bedroom door: DO NOT ENTER WITHOUT PERMISSION. Eileen's mother assumed that message was meant for Eileen's younger brothers, not her. So she continued to walk in without knocking, as she always had done. Usually her intrusions were simply met with a glare. But one day when she entered she was shocked to see her daughter examining her genitals in front of the mirror. Humiliated, Eileen screamed at her mother and refused to talk to her for days.

Privacy is important to everyone, and especially to teenagers. In the individual's quest for separateness, a place apart from everyone else—whether the physical sanctuary of one's own room or a tiny corner of the brain where a person's innermost and most intimate thoughts will never see the light of day—is crucial.

I often see parents who confess to reading their daughter's diary or listening in on their son's phone conversation. While their intentions are often honorable, their methods leave something to be desired. You value your own privacy—why not value the privacy of your child? That's part of accepting the teenager as an individual with a separate life to lead.

THE REBEL WITHOUT A CAUSE

Alex, enrolled in a private boys' prep school, was the classic rebel. He bleached his hair white, added a few pink stripes for interest, and combed in enough mousse to make it stand on end; the result made him look like he had just seen a ghost. Unlike the majority of students, whose tastes ran toward oxford shirts and khaki pants, Alex favored leather and boots with chains. While his classmates typically spent after-school hours on the basketball court, Alex's idea of a good time was to play air guitar in front of a video of the Talking Heads. On weekends he and his friends would hang out, smoking dope and drinking beer.

Most teenagers are not outward rebels. They want to be and will go to great lengths to be like everyone else their age. Rather, the rebellion is internal: a clash between the old identity (Mom and Dad's kid) and the emerging one (separate personhood).

Some kids, however, are like Alex. They "act out" their fears. Delinquency, anger, and rebellion are often the result. By rebelling, these kids are kept so busy that they don't have to take the time to confront the inner beast of uncertainty and fear. It takes a lot of energy to be angry at the world, energy that might otherwise have to be unleashed against emotions that the adolescent feels unable or unwilling to confront.

GOING SOLO

Think back to the days when your teenager was little. Remember when you were the center of his or her world. Things seemed so much easier then. You made virtually all your child's decisions. Little hurts magically disappeared with the soothing salve of your touch. Your child basked in the love, stability, and self-esteem that you were able to instill. You were a hero. The prettiest mother, the handsomest father. Strong, brilliant, all-knowing.

If you are the parent of a young child, enjoy it while you can. Invariably the day comes in every parent's life when that dependent child pushes you away and says, "Leave me alone. I want to do it myself."

Adolescents are embarrassed about dependency. They equate independence with being adult: "If you still need your parents, you're not ready to be a grownup."

This is a difficult time. For 13 years, Sharon's self-esteem came from her parents. They told her she was pretty, and she believed them. Their praise after a good report card was the fuel she needed to try even harder. They set the rules and she followed with little protest. When she started junior high, things changed. Now it seemed babyish to care so much about her parents. She wanted to pick out her own clothes. She cut the long blond hair that her parents had always admired . . . and then cried when she saw the hurt look on her mother's face. Part of her wanted to escape; the other part wanted to go back to the days when she was their good little girl.

The person in the throes of adolescence sits on a yoyo, first soaring toward freedom, next spinning back home again. One minute your adolescent can't stand to be around you, and the next minute she's insulted because you're going out to dinner without her.

Push-pull. Up-down. So goes adolescence. Psychologist Erik Erikson used the term "straw men" to describe a psychological device teens use to cope with their conflicting needs for separation and for security. According to this theory, the teenager's superego or conscience represents the adored and powerful parents of childhood. In order for the adolescent to separate successfully, he must knock the parents, or "straw men," off their pedestals.

Do you remember when you discovered that your parents were not gods but just regular people, with faults and frailties like everyone else? One mother confided in me how humiliated she had felt when her daughter saw her return from a cocktail party a little tipsy. This woman had always preached against overindulgence, and her children had never seen her drink more than a glass of wine with dinner. When the 16-year-old daughter saw her mother stumble in the door, she shook her head in disgust and called her a hypocrite.

A FRIEND IN NEED

Leigh grimaced as she stared at her face in the mirror. To her dissatisfied eyes, her hair was lank and dishwater blond, her nose was large enough to launch a ship, and her skin was blemished and sallow. Her mother assured her she was very pretty. "What do you know about it?" Leigh snapped. "You're my mother. You *have* to think that."

After years of relying on Mom and Dad for her sense of self-worth, this teen suddenly feels that their opinions carry approximately the weight of a feather. In the quest for separateness, this is inevitable. Up to a certain point, the child's sense of self-esteem comes from the parents. Then suddenly it hardly matters what they think.

But at this juncture the adolescent has not yet developed the inner confidence to tell herself, I think I'm pretty good, and probably everyone else thinks so, too. Instead there is a void that must be filled.

Where, then, does the adolescent go to fill this seemingly bottomless pit with good feelings about herself? Friends are the logical solution to the problem. Never before and never again will friends be as desperately important as they are during adolescence.

True, teenage friendships may sometimes be superficial and self-serving. Hilary is a good example of the friend an adult wouldn't want. Her barometer for friendship is whether someone is in the "right" crowd. Since the designation of "in" at her high school tends to shift like the weather, she usually drifts every few months. For a while she hung out with the cheerleaders. Then she got close to the drama set. A few months later she was an entrenched member of the student government clique. Once she made the change, previous "best" friends were ignored, their secrets divulged and disseminated throughout the school.

Not all kids are as fickle as Hilary. But some teenagers view friendship as a means to an end, a way to achieve a feeling of self-worth. If our friends are hot stuff, then so are we.

As a person matures and develops her own identity, she begins to gain confidence. She learns that she's a pretty special person regardless of whom she hangs out with. When this happens, friendships take on a new importance. Friends are selected on the basis of mutual interests and values, not their weight on the high school social scale.

COPING WITH THE WORLD

There are three main thoroughfares through adolescence.

Scott took the high road. He was a good student, had lots of friends, and even got along with his parents, aside from a few minor clashes. For him, adolescence was relatively painless and provided a smooth transition into adulthood.

Brian, like most teenagers, was on the middle track. He had his share of both successes and turmoil. A solid B student, Brian wanted to go to Harvard and studied hard for the As that would help get him there. But despite his efforts, he couldn't quite make the grades. Sometimes he was depressed over what he saw as his inadequacy. Eventually, though, he learned to make the most of his strengths, and was accepted into a good college where he thrived.

Keith took the low road through his teenage years. For him, adolescence was a time filled with turmoil. He felt ugly and stupid, so to compensate he began taking drugs. Put him and his alcoholic father in the same room and you had all the ingredients for a good fight. In short, Keith was unhappy. He wore his unhappiness like a bulletproof vest against a world that seemed to belong to everyone but him.

Adolescence, like menopause, is a transition from one plateau of life to another. It's a time to pull away from the shores of childhood and wade into the deeper waters of responsible adulthood. During the transition process, the teenager gradually adjusts to growth, development, and change.

We've talked about how difficult it is to be a teenager and why this is so. It's my belief that adolescence is, by definition, a tumultuous time for many people. Even so, most kids, like Scott and Brian, make it through without self-destruction.

Some major studies have found that most so-called "normal" teenagers have an easy adolescence. In one study, Dr. Daniel Offer studied teenagers from ten high schools in the United States and found that the vast majority were happy, fulfilled, and definitely enjoying being teenagers.

The study found that most teens:

- Do not feel inferior.
- Do not feel that others treat them badly.
- Are proud of their bodies.
- Feel in control of most situations.
- Make friends fairly easily.
- Are not afraid of sexual feelings.
- Have no major problems with their parents.
- Are optimistic about their future.

The majority of these adolescents said they were coping just fine in their world. The only problem they noted was anxiety in specific situations, such as before an important test or a date.

Although I do not disagree with Dr. Offer's research, I don't believe adolescence for most kids is one big joyride. True, the majority of teenagers manage to get through these years without stealing cars, mugging people, or becoming addicts. But in spite of outward appearances, there is a measure of inner turmoil—and there *should* be. The struggle to find one's self is never truly easy.

I can speak from experience. As a teenager I was the

quintessential "good" boy. Good student. Loving son. School leader. On the surface, I had it all covered. Inside, though, I was churning with doubt and even despair. What would I do with my life? Could I ever live up to my parents' expectations? Did I even want to? I got through it without falling apart, as most kids do. But no one can ever convince me that adolescence was the best part of *my* life!

Unfortunately, some teens do falter. Dr. Offer found that life for 20 percent of "normal" teens (those not being treated for psychiatric problems) is painful, sometimes excruciatingly so.

These kids are not coping well. They may see life as empty of purpose, a meaningless walk down a corridor to nowhere. Depression is a common problem among American teenagers, afflicting an estimated 3.4 million kids. Regrettably, it's a condition that is often ignored. Only about half of depressed teenagers get the professional help they so badly need.

EXPERIMENTATION WITH DRUGS, SEX, AND ALCOHOL

Your son arrives home late one night with beer on his breath.

You walk into your house after work and detect the pungent odor of marijuana.

While putting laundry away in your daughter's drawer, you discover a package of birth control pills.

As the parent of a teenager, even a so-called "normal" one, there's a good chance that you will experience at least one of the above scenarios or something in the same vein.

In an effort to belong, to be part of the crowd, teenagers will do almost anything. Experimentation with drugs, alcohol, and/or sex is common.

One study done in 1984 showed, in fact, that at least 30 percent of high school students were coaxed into trying that first cigarette or drink by friends. The main factors that tended to work against this friendly persuasion were strong religious convictions, staunch conservatism, and college plans.

A teenager also will join in doing something because he thinks everyone else is doing it, regardless of how untrue that is. Also, experimenting with the forbidden is an expected and necessary part of growing up.

Why do some kids choose drugs for their experimentation? It may be no more than a cultural phenomenon. Why do some go on to become alcoholics or drug addicts? That's another story. There's evidence that true addicts have a biological predisposition toward dependency on one or more mood-altering chemicals.

Today, drugs are the number one concern of most parents and of society as a whole. This plague that has infected families throughout the country cuts across all socioeconomic groups, black and white, young and not so young. Again, peer pressure is at work.

Ask Tony. For months he said no to drugs. His fast friends would smoke pot or snort cocaine in front of him, but Tony shook his head. Then a girl he liked got into the act. She could never like a guy who was afraid to get high, she told him. That crumbled Tony's resolve. He did a line of cocaine and liked it—a lot.

Ninety percent of kids in high school have smoked marijuana at least once—60 percent between sixth and ninth grades. That essentially means that the chances that your teen will go through adolescence drug-free are pretty low. This is not to say that your son or daughter is destined to become a drug addict. The majority of teenagers do not become drug addicts or even use drugs on a regular basis. In Chapter 7, we'll take a more detailed look at the drug problem and how it relates to behavior and conduct disorder.

Jill and her crowd were not into drugs. She was a cheerleader, and was elected homecoming queen. Her good grades earned her acceptance to several top colleges. You might think these substantial successes would go to her head, but in fact Jill was a nice kid, sweet and kind, well-liked by everyone. Would it surprise you to hear that at age 17 Jill had already had sexual intercourse? Since losing her virginity at the beginning of her sophomore year, she'd had three boy-friends with whom she'd had sexual relations.

Teenagers have strong sexual feelings. Think back on your own high school days. Remember what it was like when the one you thought you would love forever kissed you. Probably every fiber in your body pulsed with the intoxicating throb of desire. For that matter, even kissing someone you knew you'd only love for that evening wasn't half bad.

The teenagers of today haven't changed in that regard. They still romanticize, and they still have strong sexual desires. What *has* changed is that today a substantial number of high school students appear to be acting on those urges. In a study of two suburban high schools in 1984, Dr. Offer found that by age 17, 37 percent of girls and 54 percent of boys had had sex. I don't want to suggest that having sex during the teen years is necessarily related to psychological disturbance. For many kids, a certain amount of sexual activity is part of normal adoles-cence. It's sex at a very early age that may spell trouble. In the study just mentioned, the major factors that tended to inhibit very early sexual experience were a happy and supportive household in which both parents were present, and a steady history of academic success. Probably these teenagers were less likely to have frequent early sexual intercourse because they often looked to their families for gratification and support, and also because they were so busy studying to get good grades that they didn't have the time for an overactive social life.

WHO AM I?

Psychiatrists recognize four basic "tasks" that are crucial to normal adolescent development. These are:

1. Separating from parents and the family.
2. Growing into new, independents relationships.
3. Learning to love.
4. Learning to work.

In the eternal quest to discover the answer to the question "Who am I?" the adolescent is a little like a chef trying to create a new dish. A little of this, a lot of that, maybe a pinch of this. Sometimes the dish flops, and it's back to the mixing bowl.

What results from this creativity—and I believe it is the most creative thing we ever do—is the person we ultimately become. Sometime during this process that we call adolescence, a definite path emerges. It may take ten years or more, but most of us learn during this testing time what our strengths are. Then we put those strengths to positive use in the form of a career. We learn what makes us laugh and what we find revolting. We fine-tune our sense of right and wrong. We learn the power we have over those who like or love us. Ideally, we also learn how not to abuse that power.

The road has its twists and turns—more for some than for others—but in following these personal, individual curves we eventually reach the end of our own journey toward adulthood.

As your teenager begins to forge his or her identity, there will be days when you wonder where you went wrong. For some parents, the rebellion, the pulling away, is a bitter pill to swallow. You will undoubtedly find yourself wondering on more than one occasion, Is this normal? Does my teenager have an emotional problem?

Let's change the direction of our discussion at this point and turn our attention to abnormal adolescent behavior.

Chapter 3

Why Do Things Go Wrong?

"They didn't let me go out very often, as each time I returned beaten up by the street urchins. But fighting was my only pleasure and I gave myself up to it body and soul.

Mother would flog me with a strap, but the punishment only put me in a worse rage and the next time I fought even more violently and as a result was punished more severely. And then I warned mother that if she didn't stop beating me I would bite her hand and run away into the fields to freeze. This made her push me from her in amazement, and she walked up and down the room, her breath coming in weary gasps, and said, 'little beast!'

That living, throbbing gamut of feelings called love slowly faded in me and in its place there flared up, more and more often, smoldering blue fires of ill-will against everyone."
—Maxim Gorky, *My Childhood*, 1915

Most of the parents of conduct-disordered kids that I see are a lot like the mother of this famous Russian writer. They feel they're at the end of their rope, worn to the very nub of their resolve. All they can do is shake their heads and wonder, Why?

Why? is a difficult question to answer. There are numerous theories. Some blame conduct disorders on psychological factors. For example, if a boy steals, one explanation may be that his overly harsh superego has created intolerable guilt, which he attempts to relieve with punishment-provoking be-havior. Others cast responsibility for persistent unacceptable behavior on a hostile environment. The girl who sleeps with anyone, anytime, does so because she's had an unloving and unsupervised home life. Then there are the biological theo-ries that postulate there is something—no one knows precisely what—in the genetic makeup of a kid with conduct disorder that causes abnormal behavior. In other words, something is neurologically amiss.

If your child had pneumonia, I could pinpoint the specific bacteria causing the illness. I could show you a dozen other patients with the same pneumonia, and tell you that your son or daughter's treatment would be identical.

Unfortunately, in the realm of psychiatric disturbances—specifically, conduct disorders—things are rarely so simple.

Every kid who enters my program enters through a differ-ent door. You can't put them all into one basket. There is no single reason why kids do drugs, steal, or get into trouble. True, the behaviors may be identical. Dan and Josh both have run away, done drugs, and been caught stealing cars. Both are conduct-disordered. But Dan was basically a normal kid until his parents' divorce, when he was on the edge of adolescence, knocked him for a loop. Josh, on the other hand, was never a stranger to trouble, whether it was on the neighborhood playground, at school, or the home front. The same type of behavior, yes. But the roots of the problem sit deeper within Josh.

If you gain anything from reading this chapter, it should be that no two kids with conduct disorder are the same—no matter how similar they may seem at first. It's also impossi-ble to generalize about causes. Although some studies have hypothesized that extremely violent people have an extra Y chromosome, we have yet to identify a specific gene or biochemical substance responsible for conduct disorder. This is not to say we'll never identify a biological cause. Remem-ber, it wasn't so long ago that we blamed depression solely on faulty parenting during the early years. Now, we know that many people who are severely depressed have a malfunction of the brain's chemical messengers.

So, I cannot tell you that your son Donald, who raped a 10-year-old neighbor girl, did so because of a defective gene. That would be too easy. I can tell you, however, that in the past fifteen or twenty years, psychiatrists have found that more and more emotional disturbances and behavior problems seem to have a biological or neurological link. There is something in an individual's biological make-up that, when mixed with certain environmental stresses, predisposes him or her to certain types of behavior. This predisposition interacts with the individual's emotional, social, and psychological environment to produce a kid with a conduct disorder.

ANTS IN HIS PANTS

Jerry was a kid who couldn't stop moving. Getting him to sit down even at mealtimes was like trying to put a saddle on a wild mustang. School was a disaster. He was constantly on the principal's bench, and he had the dubious distinction of never having earned a grade above a D. Jerry's father's solution to the problems of this kid who wouldn't listen to anyone was to administer severe beatings with his belt, usually at the rate of one or two a day. Not surprisingly, Jerry's behavior didn't improve. In fact, it got worse.

This is a good example of how several factors come into play. Jerry had what is known as *attention deficit disorder*, or what we used to call hyperactivity, a condition whose roots are probably neurological. Typically, kids with this disorder seem to "bounce off the walls" much of the time. It's not hard to understand why they do poorly in school. If you can't sit still long enough to concentrate, how can you learn? So instead of learning, Jerry, who has an extremely poor self-image because of his "stupidity," causes trouble. His family punishes him severely, which reinforces his image of himself as a "bad" kid. All this combines to shape the way his mind views the world and his place in it.

Jerry is a good example of a kid with a biological problem that has led to conduct disorder. Carla, who has a bipolar (manic-depressive) illness, is another one whose neurological makeup has contributed to severe behavior problems. One day she is so depressed she can't get out of bed in the morning. On another day she feels so high she can't sleep at all. In her moments of depression, she's attempted suicide and used drugs. In her bouts of mania she's totaled her father's car, stolen her mother's credit cards, and gambled away some family heirlooms.

But hyperactivity and manic-depressive illness aren't the only possible biological contributors to conduct disorder. Perhaps you remember Marcus Welby, M.D., television's quintessential purveyor of medical wisdom. Once every season or so, Dr. Welby was faced with a perplexing case of a nice young man from a fine family who occasionally went on violent rampages. At some point in the hour, something clicked, and Dr. Welby would diagnose temporal lobe epilepsy, a sort of misfiring of the brain that causes sporadic outbursts of violence.

Unlike the world of television where everything occurs in its most obvious form, this condition rarely presents itself so neatly. While I can't say that I see a lot of kids with conduct disorders who have been diagnosed as having temporal lobe epilepsy, I can tell you that many of the kids I treat with conduct disorders have what we call impulse control disorder. This involves rash and impulsive behavior that may or may not be violent. What causes it? I don't know, but I do know that it sometimes responds to Tegretol, a medication used to treat temporal lobe epilepsy.

Whatever the origin of impulse control disorder, Randy has it. Randy is a 16-year-old who has been undergoing treatment in my program. One day recently he appeared wearing an earring, a behavior that wasn't allowed. When a counselor asked him to remove it, he refused. Then he put it in his mouth. As punishment, he was put in seclusion for a brief time. When I asked Randy for the earring, he started cursing and threatening me. This violent response to a minor incident is typical of the kid with an impulse control problem.

UNHAPPY HOMES

I wrote before that I rarely see conduct-disordered kids from stable, loving homes.

This isn't to imply that many of the parents of these kids are not trying to provide a stable and supportive environment. But somewhere along the line, something has gone awry.

Many of the kids I see have been allowed to run wild without any parental supervision. Then, when they do get caught misbehaving, the parents administer punishment that borders on the brutal. Physical and even sexual abuse is not uncommon in these families. Parental alcoholism, depression, and other emotional problems are often evident. Sometimes it seems that the parents actually encourage their kids to act out, because they themselves sometimes get so angry that they inadvertently teach their kids the opposite of the golden rule.

While you might expect behavior problems to occur in families living in poverty, the middle and upper classes are by no means exempt from conduct disorder's spreading tentacles.

Justin, a kid who was recently in the program, came from a family whose income was well into six figures. His dad was a successful banker and his mother a professor at a local college. Both were on the fast track, working twelve-hour days, toting bulging briefcases that kept them busy and preoccupied even when they were home. Justin was the kid who seemed to have everything: a beautiful home, plenty of cash, lots of freedom. But even though Justin had his own BMW parked in the driveway, his hobby was stealing expensive foreign cars for joyriding.

WHEN DAD LEAVES FOR GOOD

Caitlin, like many of the kids with conduct disorders, comes from a broken home. Her father walked out when she was in first grade, and never came back. Her mother, preoccupied with her own loneliness and depression, began going out to bars at night. Every morning when Caitlin woke up it seemed there was a different man at the breakfast table. When she was 12, Caitlin started having sex with anyone who could pay for it.

An estimated 20 percent of all children under the age of 18 (more than 50 percent of black children) do not live with their fathers. Are these kids more likely to develop conduct disorders? I believe so. Kids who live in families without a father seem particularly likely to display the kind of behavior that gets them in trouble with the law, and as a result—if they're lucky—into a treatment program.

However, at least one preliminary study indicates that it appears that even more important than the presence of a father is how much supervision the mother is able to give. In a study of 12- to 17-year-olds, investigators found that teenagers who had a strong mother who maintained control and supervision after the father left were no more likely to get into trouble than kids from two-parent homes. The problem is that many divorced women running households are not able to maintain adequate supervision.

A family disrupted because of death rather than divorce appears less likely to produce a child with a conduct disorder. This suggests that it's not the breakup of the home per se, but the family discord preceding the breakup, that is related to a kid getting into trouble.

Divorce, while a sad fact of life, need not drive a kid over the edge. In my experience of working with conduct-disordered kids and their families, I've found that it is not the divorce itself that causes a snap in the taut strings of a kid's behavior. Rather, it's how the divorce is handled. Please don't misunderstand me. There is no doubt that divorce is traumatic for everyone involved. But kids are resilient creatures. And divorce, when handled properly, is not enough to crumble the structure of a sound personality.

A large percentage of the kids who end up in my program are the victims of divorce. I say victims, because often these kids do not belong to a "successfully" divorced couple. How do I define a successful divorce? It's one in which the ex-partners make an effort to maintain a polite if not warm relationship. Both parents continue to have a strong relationship with the children. Discipline has been maintained. Dad doesn't bad-mouth Mom, and Mom never talks against Dad.

Rather, what I usually see are the kids of parents who are *themselves* acting out. Take Joan and Henry. They're the parents of Beth, a girl who at 17 has had three pregnancies.

Married right after high school, Joan and Henry always had a turbulent relationship. Beth remembers lying in bed as a little girl, head under the covers, in an attempt to drown out her parents' shouting. For weeks everything would be okay. Then Henry would drink too much, come home mad, and the threats and accusations would send Beth cowering into her canopied bed. When she was 12, her parents split up.

It was a bitter divorce. Both fought for custody of Beth, and Henry lost. Some days it seemed all Beth heard was how bad her father was. When Beth was with her father, he rarely stopped criticizing his ex-wife. Beth rarely said a word in defense of either parent, but inside she was screaming, Stop it. Leave me out of this. Two years after the divorce, Henry lost his job and stopped sending monthly support checks. This was the chance Joan was waiting for. She refused to let him see their daughter.

A year later Joan remarried. Her new husband was a career Army sergeant who used the same iron-fisted discipline with his new family as he did with his recruits. Six months after the wedding, Beth ran away. When she reluctantly returned more than eighteen months later, she'd already had three abortions, was using crack as often as she could get it, and had been arrested for shoplifting.

Most of the kids I treat tell me that after their parents' divorce, they felt displaced. Sometimes a surrogate parent moves in before the ink is dry on the divorce papers. In addition to the difficulty of adjusting to the new father figure, there may be new siblings vying for attention. Even under the best of circumstances, with a stepparent who could give the parents on *The Brady Bunch* a run for their money, the going is usually rough at first.

How rough? That depends on which reports you read. In one study of violent boys with conduct disorder who had been successfully treated, a factor in the success of their treatment appeared to be a strong stepfather. Many of the natural fathers were themselves alcoholics and/or antisocial personalities, whereas the stepfathers were not. In these cases, the stepfather had a positive influence.

However, the opposite effect is also possible. Even a well-meaning stepfather has to tread lightly when dealing with his wife's children from a former marriage: He's an intruder in the kids' lives, and he needs to give them time to get used to him. If he isn't particularly well-meaning—i.e., if he charges in with insensitive criticism, or mistreats the mother, or favors one child over another—he may become not part of the solution, but part of the problem.

IF IT'S TUESDAY, THIS MUST BE OMAHA

Penny was an Army brat. By the time she was 14, her family had moved nine times. In the early years, moving didn't seem to affect Penny adversely. But when she entered junior high, things changed. "I no sooner made a friend than I had to leave and go through the whole process again," Penny told me. "I got so I didn't want to have anyone I'd have to say goodbye to." Lonely and depressed, Penny started skipping school. Then she ran away.

Moving is hard for anyone. For a teenager, it can be devastating. A person in the midst of adolescent tumult needs the comfort of the familiar: school, neighborhood, friends. To be suddenly uprooted is to be cut off from necessary support systems. The result for many teens is depression, which may lead to drug abuse and other problems.

True, if your kid has had a solid and positive experience with life thus far, he isn't going to suddenly turn into Jack the Ripper because you pack up the car and move from Orlando to Oklahoma City. But a move that leaves him friendless and unsure of life can cause your former bookworm to turn into a truant. Behavior changes—some major and usually not for the better—are common when an adolescent is forced to move.

Many parents, caught up in their own stress and sense of guilt over uprooting the family, choose to ignore the early signs of trouble. Instead of sharing with their teenager their own fears and worries about moving, they usually try to accentuate the positive. "Oh, you'll love it. Stop complaining. The new school will be great." This only serves to broaden the parent-child gap. What's going to fill up the emptiness? If friends are no longer around, maybe drugs will do the job.

PROBLEMS ASSOCIATED WITH CONDUCT DISORDER

Conduct disorder does not discriminate. It occurs in black and white families, rich and poor, around the country clubs of suburbia and on the gritty, crowded sidewalks of the ghetto.

Some kids with conduct disorder literally don't know where their next meal is coming from. Others have Olympic-sized pools in the backyard and closets full of designer clothes. Many have extremely high IQs; some are of average or below-average intelligence.

Despite these outward differences, a large percentage of these kids share a common bond: they all come from basically dysfunctional families. Whether home is a one-room apartment in a roach-infested welfare hotel or a twenty-room villa on a landscaped estate, something has usually gone awry in the family.

Let's talk about some of the common problems that I frequently see in the families of these kids.

ONE MORE DRINK FOR THE ROAD

Jamie's dad was an alcoholic, but not the kind you see lying on the sidewalk, clutching a bottle of cheap wine in a brown paper bag. His father had a responsible job as a construction foreman, and never touched a drop while he was at work. But after work he would pull the plug on his self-restraint and devote his considerable energies to downing a quart of bourbon. It was always, "One more drink, then I'll get home to the family." Jamie rarely saw his father sober. When he was 10, his dad offered him a drink. By the time Jamie was 13, he was an alcoholic.

Numerous studies have documented a high incidence of alcoholism among the parents, particularly the fathers, of kids with conduct disorders. Many of these alcoholic fathers are also antisocial, and a substantial number have a history of aggression, arrest, and imprisonment.

Generally speaking, the kids with the most aggressive conduct disorders—those who have been arrested for committing violent crimes—have fathers who show similar behavior.

What about the mothers? Unfortunately, many of the mothers of kids with conduct disorders also have substantial problems. In one study, researchers found that mothers whose children were diagnosed with conduct disorder were more likely to be depressed, exhibit antisocial behavior, have hysteria, or abuse alcohol or drugs.

SEXUAL AND PHYSICAL ABUSE

Gina is a pretty girl with long black hair and skin the color of milk. When I met her, she also had a black eye, a split lip, and a trail of bruises down her legs. Arrested for trying to steal a radio, Gina matter-of-factly explained to me that her father had beat her up when he found out she was sleeping with a friend of his. It wasn't the first time. Records showed that she'd been hospitalized several times with numerous fractures and burns.

Parental abuse, whether physical or sexual, often goes hand-in-hand with conduct disorder. Is conduct disorder the result of child abuse? We can't say there is a causal relationship. We can say, however, that these abused children often have trouble respecting authority. Because of their traumatic life experiences, they have difficulty trusting and establishing intimate relationships with adults. And these characteristics can lead to antisocial or unacceptable behavior.

Of course, not all kids with conduct disorder have been abused. In one study of both abused and nonabused kids with conduct disorder, the factors that tended to be associated with abuse were extreme poverty, a single-parent home, a parent who was abused as a child, and depression.

TO BE A FLY ON THE WALL

Close your eyes and try to imagine what it is like to be a kid living in your home. That's what I try to do every time a new kid is admitted into my program. In a lengthy interview with the parents, I try to be the proverbial fly on the wall, examining the environment that has helped to produce a kid with a conduct disorder.

The following are a sample of the questions I ask. Read through them, remember back, and answer them as honestly as you can. Perhaps they may provide some insight.

- What is the structure of the family—who's present and who's missing?
- Who is responsible for child care?
- Who pays for it?

- What's the family's financial situation?
- If the parents are divorced, is the custodial parent maintaining a commitment to keep the children in touch with the missing parent?
- Was the divorce friendly or acrimonious?
- Tell me about your (the parents') friendships and peers.
- Describe your early years with your child.
- Describe your techniques for disciplining your child.
- What activities do you and your child participate in together?
- Tell me about your child's friends.
- What does your adolescent do in his or her spare time?
- What is your attitude about school?
- If the child brings home a good grade, what is your response?
- What about a bad grade?
- Do you kiss, hug, or show affection to your teen, and how does he respond?
- What is your attitude toward misbehavior?

A PARENT ASKS, "IS IT ALL MY FAULT?"

Life had always been easy for Deborah and Jonathan. They were both near the top of their graduating class at an Ivy League university. Jonathan joined one of the most prestigious law firms in the state, and a few years later he became the youngest partner. Deborah, an architect, traveled around the country designing office buildings and making a name for herself.

Five years to the day after they were married, their son was born.

Robert was not exactly what they had hoped for in a child. Born with a congenital eye defect, he bumped into walls until the problem was discovered when he was 3. A chubby boy whose favorite pastime was eating, Robert showed no inclination or talent for the sports at which his father excelled. Nor was he academically inclined. Throughout grade school he never made better than a C.

His parents felt compelled to re-create Robert in their own beautiful image. Deborah signed him up for a series of art lessons, which he hated. When he was 10, Jonathan sent him to a computer camp for the summer. The boy was miserable.

Viewed as somewhat of a nerd at school, Robert spent his free time in the kitchen, teaching himself to cook from his mother's cookbooks and later developing his own recipes. This pastime his parents accepted unenthusiastically, until he failed two courses during his sophomore year in high school. His punishment? No more cooking until he brought his grades up.

In a rage that seemed uncharacteristic of his usual mild temperament, Robert started a fire in the kitchen while his parents were at work. Then he swallowed a full bottle of aspirin. Two months later his parents sat in my office, torn apart with guilt.

The parents of kids with conduct disorders who I see basically fit into one of three groups.

Those in the first group refuse to acknowledge the seriousness of the problem. "He just needs a good kick in the butt to set him straight," said the father of a boy who had been mugging old ladies. This is a father who has been kicking his son in the butt for ten years, to no avail.

At the other extreme are the parents who blame themselves totally. "Jennifer's a wonderful girl. It's all my fault," says a tearful mother whose 13-year-old daughter refuses to go to school and can't stay away from drugs.

In the middle are the more reasonable parents. They acknowledge their parenting mistakes and realize that they are part, but only part, of the problem. At the same time, they understand that ultimately their child must take responsibility for his or her behavior.

Like Deborah and Jonathan, most parents I see feel guilty about what has happened. Their kid has been a disappointment— not pretty or handsome enough, fat, a poor student, a wimp instead of a star athlete, whatever. This disappointment has been conveyed, which of course deals a crushing blow to the kid's developing self-esteem. If your own mom or dad doesn't like you, who will?

One of the first things a parent has to deal with is his or her own narcissism. No, your painfully shy daughter is never going to fulfill your dream of being a great actress. So what? That's your dream, not hers. She loves to sit by herself and write poetry. Some parents join groups such as Parents Anonymous, to help them cope with their guilt and confront their disappointments.

PULLING THE TRIGGER

Why now? After all these years, why is my son suddenly stealing, lying, and skipping school?

As I've said before and really want to stress, adolescence is normally a time of tumult, even under the best of circumstances. When I'm evaluating a new kid, I look at the major areas of his or her life. In the past, was the kid functioning well at school, at home, with friends? If after years of smooth sailing he suddenly goes off the deep end, this may be just an extreme response to a particularly trying period of adolescence. Suddenly, for the first time in his life, there is a real opportunity to act out. He has shed the yoke of parental restraint. Away from your prying eyes, your adolescent is free to drive a car, have sex, take drugs, drink. Some teens act out to an extreme.

Does a basically sound teen who gets into trouble need treatment? Yes. Is his conduct disorder as severe as that of the kid who has always been in trouble? Probably not. All conduct disorders are not created equal.

In this chapter we've talked about the causes of conduct disorder and looked at factors that can contribute to its development. But not all antisocial behavior can be attributed to conduct disorder. Several psychiatric conditions can either stand alone or occur in concert with a conduct disorder. Let's go on to learn about them now.

Chapter 4

When Is It Not Conduct Disorder?

A boy can't seem to sit still in class. A girl begins to sleep fourteen hours a day or starve herself down to an eighty-five-pound skeleton.

In this chapter, we will look at some disorders commonly seen in adolescents. Some, like attention deficit disorder and depression, are frequently found in kids with conduct disorder.

ATTENTION DEFICIT DISORDER WITH/WITHOUT HYPERACTIVITY

When your teenager was a young child, did he show any of the following symptoms?

- Often fidgets with hands or feet or squirms in his seat
- Cannot seem to remain seated
- Is easily distracted
- Has trouble waiting his or her turn at games
- Often blurts out answers before the questions are complete

- Has trouble following instructions
- Does not complete projects
- Has trouble paying attention
- Has a problem playing quietly
- Often talks excessively
- Often interrupts or intrudes on others
- Does not listen closely
- Often loses school materials
- Often participates in dangerous activities

For a child who shows at least eight of these characteristics, the American Psychiatric Association criteria suggest a diagnosis of attention deficit disorder (ADD), which may occur either with or without hyperactivity.

ADD is a problem affecting at least 5 percent of all school-age children. The precise cause is unknown, but it is thought to be a neurological abnormality or a combination of several such abnormalities.

In 60 to 70 percent of all cases, parents begin noticing the telltale signs of ADD by the time their child is 2 years old. It's possible to make a diagnosis by 4 or 5 years of age. Although the child may outgrow hyperactivity, one study has shown that about one-third of kids with this disorder continue to show some signs of it in adulthood.

Almost from day one, Ben was a little terror. As a toddler he had severe temper tantrums and got into constant mischief. Taking Ben shopping was an open invitation to disaster. He caused seemingly willful damage to store displays, and sometimes his parents ended up paying for ruined merchandise. From early morning until late at night, Ben was in constant motion. Supervising him was an exhausting task. His mother knew her son was more "hyper" than the average child, but she felt defensive when anyone criticized Ben's behavior. She rationalized that "boys will be boys." She thought school might calm him down and give him some discipline, but in fact it only brought out the worst in him. Midway through second grade, Ben was diagnosed as having attention-deficit disorder *with* hyperactivity (ADDH).

GO TO THE BACK OF THE CLASS

Typically, the kid with ADDH is a troublemaker in school. Unable to concentrate long enough to complete an assignment, he tends to bounce around the classroom like a rubber ball. A teacher will often complain that one of these children in a classroom takes more of her time and attention than the twenty-five other kids put together.

Like Ben, Andy had problems in school from the very first day. He was the kid who just couldn't seem to get things right. Unlike Ben, however, Andy was not disruptive. He didn't run around wildly or bombard his fellow classmates with paper airplanes. Rather, he would sit placidly. Even when he was staring intently at an assignment, he couldn't concentrate on the problem at hand. At the age of 10, Andy was diagnosed as having attention deficit disorder *without* hyperactivity (ADD).

Although there are certainly kids with attention deficit disorder who never have severe behavioral problems, a high percentage develop conduct disorder during adolescence. Most of the kids with attention deficit disorder that I see are also hyperactive. Because they're so impulsive, they are more likely to be aggressive than conduct-disordered kids without ADDH.

Why do many kids with ADDH grow into adolescents with conduct disorder?

Let's look at Brian. He always had problems relating to people. He couldn't sit still long enough for anyone to get to know him. In school, he spent more time racing up and down the rows in his classroom than sitting at his desk. He was fidgety, agitated, and always interrupting the teacher. At first she thought he was making a bid for her approval, so she made a point of calling on him often. But since Brian hadn't been paying attention, he never knew the answer. It wasn't long before the other kids started calling him "Dummy."

At home, Brian's parents showed their concern by firmly insisting he sit still and do his homework. Usually he would start to comply, but then give up after a few minutes. He didn't mean to be a bad boy—he just couldn't apply himself to any one thing for long. His dad's response was to take off his belt and use it on Brian's backside.

And so it went. For years Brian heard that he was dumb, lazy, and goofy, and gradually his self-esteem flattened like a pancake. But since he had a lot of spark in him, he managed to lash back at the world by getting into trouble.

I met Brian when he was 15. He had dropped out of school, been arrested for auto theft, and was using drugs heavily. I started him on Ritalin, a psychostimulant medication that's often helpful in treating ADD. As an inpatient at Laurel Oaks, Brian responded swiftly and dramatically to medication and therapy. Within a couple of weeks he made major improvements in his ability to relate to his family and to other kids.

It's not hard to see how a youngster who has never felt successful can turn into a problem. Combine this with the energy and impulsivity of many of these children, and you have an ideal mix of ingredients for a conduct-disordered kid.

I'd like to add a word here about the medication that helped Brian. Ritalin has received bad press for many years. It started when reporters discovered some schools in which an alarmingly large number of children were receiving Ritalin, sometimes at the request of teachers. This painted a somber, Brave New World picture of kids being drugged into passivity and conformity. A public outcry developed, and as a result many intelligent and educated people are still leery of Ritalin.

No doubt some doctors do overprescribe Ritalin. However, that doesn't make this medication useless. My experience is that when it is given in appropriate doses to children with certain definite symptoms, Ritalin is a very valuable aid to treatment. It can help a hyperactive child calm down enough to function normally and be happy with herself and other children.

EARLY TREATMENT

In most cases, a key to prevention of future trouble is early diagnosis of an attention-deficit disorder. If Brian's problem had been diagnosed during his early school years, he could have been treated with medication and psychotherapy (both one-to-one counseling and family therapy) to check his symptoms. His whole school experience would have been entirely different—less chaotic, more positive—and his family life would have been smoother. Under these circumstances, he might never have developed a need to act out negative feelings.

"LEARNING DISABILITIES"

A kid with a learning disability has what you might visualize as a short circuit within her brain. This neurological "wiring problem" drastically cuts down on her ability to process certain kinds of information efficiently. Let's say she habitually confuses certain letters: "b" and "p," for example, or "m" and "w." Of course, all young children who are learning to read have these problems to a certain extent. But this particular child, even if she is alert and intelligent, needs an unusual amount of practice and repetition before her mind automatically recognizes these differences between letters. If no one notices her problem, the result may be frustration, poor grades, and a plummeting sense of self-worth.

In recent years, the "learning disability" diagnosis has been somewhat overused. Often both schools and parents find it easier to blame a child's academic problems on a neurophysiological abnormality than on emotional or social issues.

Very rarely is the diagnosis of a learning disorder specific.

For example, dyslexia is a general term that simply means difficulty in reading. It says nothing about where in the brain the problem may be occurring. Sometimes neurological tests can help pinpoint the source of a learning difficulty.

The following are some common problems that may interfere with a child's ability to learn in school:

Developmental reading, writing, expressive language, and arithmetic disorders: Occasionally a child of normal intelligence will have a severe problem learning to read, write, speak clearly, or do arithmetic. "Dyslexia," a catch-all term for reading problems, falls into this category. Often developmental problems can be overcome, but it takes patient teaching and lots of practice. Early diagnosis is important to prevent the child from falling too far behind her classmates.

Communications disorders: Speech and language problems can range from pronunciation difficulties to severe stuttering. Speech therapy is usually very effective.

Hearing impairment: This may be congenital or the result of an infection or an accident. Even a mild hearing impairment can keep a child from learning. An ear specialist can diagnose and treat the problem.

Vision impairment: A child who cannot focus clearly on the blackboard or the book in front of her will not progress in school as readily as she should. Children as young as age 3 should be checked for amblyopia, an eye-muscle problem that if left untreated can eventually lead to loss of sight in one eye.

A fair number of the kids in my program have learning problems that hindered their academic progress through years of schooling. An untreated disability, which usually robs the child of self-esteem, can contribute powerfully to inappropriate impulsivity and self-destructive behavior patterns.

DEPRESSION

Grownups aren't the only ones capable of suffering from clinical depression; teenagers, too, are vulnerable. Common symptoms of teenage depression include the following:

- Loss of interest in things that were once a source of enjoyment
- A long-term change in mood
- An increase in the amount of time spent sleeping
- Weight loss or weight gain
- Movement disturbances—for instance, going from lethargic in the morning to agitated in the afternoon
- Guilty feelings, which may be manifested by sadness, withdrawal, self-reproach, or obsessions
- Talk of suicide or death

Although there are a million reasons why a kid may be depressed, there's only one basic reason: the teenager is struggling with issues of independence. Much of the time she is busy trying to pull away from the nest. At other times, though, something inside is like a magnet pulling her back— she feels that if she turns away from her parents she'll lose her innocence, her spontaneity, maybe even her likability. Coping with the loss of childhood—the loss of parents as "caretakers"—is perhaps the biggest task of adolescence. Becoming responsibly independent isn't easy. The resulting feelings of confusion and emptiness are a major ingredient in teenage depression.

Then, too, the fragility of teenage friendships makes the adolescent prone to rejection. Being rejected hurts, especially when you don't have a solid feeling of self-worth to begin with.

Most of us are uncomfortable with ambivalence, and teenagers are no exception. In the teen years especially, life seems to be either extremely wonderful or else "the pits." Some teenagers get stuck on the downswing. Instead of rising back up after a setback, they keep falling into an abyss of despair.

The point is that it's normal for a teenager to be depressed—some of the time. Your daughter sits home and broods while her best friend, with a handsome escort, sails off to the prom. Your sons tries out for the football team, gets turned down, and doesn't smile for a week. The eruption of a new pimple just before the big dance, a B instead of an A in biology, a rejection letter from a certain college—to parents these problems may seem like minor annoyances, but to vulnerable teenagers they're hard to shake off.

When is depression something a parent should be concerned about? Generally, if the depression only lasts a week or so, it's probably nothing to worry about. Sometimes, however, depression seems to acquire an ugly momentum. The triggering event fades into the background, but depression itself moves in and takes over.

DEPRESSED AND ACTING OUT

Even though many kids with conduct disorder are depressed, surprisingly few of them show the classic signs and symptoms of depression: eating too much or too little, sleeping all day or waking in the wee hours of the morning, dwelling obsessively on imagined personal shortcomings, hiding out in their rooms.

Instead, they have what's known as "masked depression," which shows up as chronic difficulties in starting and maintaining positive relationships with people.

Depressed conduct-disordered kids seem to cultivate self-defeating behaviors. A girl may be promiscuous. A boy may repeatedly get himself expelled from school. Both may sneak out in the middle of the night to get high with friends. The next day they don't have enough energy to stay awake in school.

Antidepressant medications are often useful adjuncts in the

treatment of clinical depression. About 25 percent of the kids for whom I prescribe antidepressants respond dramatically with brightened mood and improved attitude. In another 25 to 50 percent, the response is more muted—mostly just a reduction in agitation and anxiety. The rest don't respond to medication at all.

BIPOLAR ILLNESS

Chelsea's moods were like a seesaw. One minute she was floating on clouds, the next she was collapsed in the dumps. A bright, attractive girl, Chelsea was involved in every activity her high school had to offer. She was a cheerleader, a homecoming princess, and a student council representative. On a good day she would literally dance through the hallways, bubbling over with enthusiasm for life. On the bad days, she wouldn't bother getting out of bed. By the time she was in her senior year, Chelsea was spending as many days alone in her bedroom as she was going to school.

Mood swings are developmentally appropriate for many adolescents. However, some teens do have what we call bipolar illness. You've probably heard it referred to as manic-depressive illness.

This disorder wears many hats. Some kids are like Chelsea, with very high highs and very low lows. Others may only be mildly depressed but have extreme bouts of wild, hyperactive behavior. Still others may get very depressed but have only mild periods of "frenzy."

Bipolar illness is not uncommon among the conduct-disordered kids I treat. During manic episodes, some kids become both aggressive and destructive. In low periods, it may be too much to get up and go to school in the morning, and this problem is eventually labeled truancy. Very depressed kids' thoughts may turn to suicide.

Teenagers with one of the varieties of bipolar illness, feeling clearly that they are overpowered by their moods, may take drugs either to pep themselves up or to calm themselves down. There's a technical name for this behavior: self-medication.

The trouble is that self-medication is usually illegal and always dangerous. Taking an antidepressant or a mood-stabilizing medication under a doctor's supervision is one thing; alternately getting high and cooling out with street drugs (or with medicine prescribed for someone else) is quite another.

The medication of choice for bipolar illness is lithium carbonate, a natural mineral salt. In 70 percent of cases, an appropriate daily dose of lithium prevents manic episodes. Tegretol, an anticonvulsant medication, may be given in conjunction with lithium—particularly if the teenager has a history of neurological problems or aggressive outbursts. Because of possible side effects, which include drowsiness, irritability, blood cell suppression, hallucinations, and gastrointestinal upsets, kid taking these medications have to be monitored carefully.

EATING DISORDERS

I don't have to tell you that being slim has become an American cultural obsession. The bathroom scale is a shrine at which many of us worship every morning. What we see on the dial has the power to buoy our self-esteem—or plunge us into self-hatred. Someone once said a woman can never be too rich or too thin. Unfortunately, many young girls today take the latter part of that message to heart. Lots of men diet, but girls and women approach the issue much more seriously. In the quest to be able to pinch less than an inch, girls often torture themselves with stringent diets.

Today, an estimated one out of every 100 girls aged 16 to 18 has an eating disorder: bulimia, the more common disorder, or anorexia nervosa. While these conditions are most often found among girls from white middle-class families, they also occur in other racial and socioeconomic groups.

BINGE AND PURGE

Rachel, a 16-year-old from a big family, was obsessed with dieting. Although her mother, who was Italian, prepared massive meals of truly mouth-watering food, Rachel wouldn't do more than pick at her plate. While the rest of the family dived into the steaming pasta, succulent veal cutlets, and tender eggplant parmesan, she'd munch on a carrot and nibble at a hard boiled egg or a scoop of cottage cheese.

Still, Rachel never lost much weight. The reason was that she regularly sneaked food. All day long she would think about what she was going to eat when she got home from school. She'd race home, throw open the cupboard doors, and gorge herself on goodies. She tried to keep things under control, but she was so hungry from starving all day that she could easily eat a whole pound of corn chips, an entire package of cream-filled cookies, or a full quart of ice cream at one sitting. It felt good to eat, but afterward the guilt was crushing. How could she wreck her diet like this? Many times, disgusted at the prospect of gaining weight and physically ill from all she had gobbled down, Rachel would stick her fingers down her throat and vomit.

THE GIRL WHO THOUGHT SHE WAS FAT

Anya began her teens with a little baby fat. Not much, but enough to make her want to do something about it. So she started dieting to lose five pounds. When she reached her goal after a couple of weeks, she looked into the mirror and decided that wasn't enough. She needed to lose another five pounds.

She began jogging five miles a day. On top of that, she cut her calorie intake in half.

Six months later, the girl who wanted to lose five pounds had lost forty. But even though she now weighed only 85 pounds, Anya still saw a fat girl every time she studied her contours in the mirror. Her parents tried to get her to eat, but Anya kept on dieting.

Anya was finally hospitalized when her weight dropped to 60 pounds, but it was too late. After so many months of starvation, her young body was severely weakened. Despite intensive treatment, Anya died of heart failure at the age of 14.

We don't see many kids with eating disorders at Laurel Oaks. These kids—almost always girls—are definitely acting out. But they're directing the action *inward* against themselves, unlike conduct-disordered kids who turn their action *outward* against others.

According to one theory, eating disorders are one way for girls to avoid dealing with their emerging sexuality. Identity problems and mood disorders may complicate the picture.

About 6 percent of anorectics die as a result of malnutrition, so treatment is very important. Hospitalization may be necessary. Successful treatment usually combines psychotherapy, behavior modification, and nutritional rehabilitation. Antidepressant medications sometimes help. The short-term success rate for treatment is about 70 percent, but 50 percent of these girls and women continue to have chronic eating difficulties or other psychiatric problems.

Interestingly, some girls with eating disorders mix well in group therapy with the brash, impulsive conduct-disordered kids. Since these girls are troubled by too much internalizing of negative feelings, they seem to loosen up when surrounded by kids who externalize their problems.

We've explored some of the problems that may occur in conduct-disordered kids. Now let's take a closer look at the kinds of behavior commonly seen in conduct disorder.

Chapter 5

Antisocial Behavior in All Its Forms

Jeremy steals school and office supplies: staplers, bottles of correction fluid, different colored pens. He has no use for most of these objects. Besides, his family is well off and he has a generous allowance; if he needed any of these things he could easily buy them.

Sixteen-year-old Alicia can't seem to stop lying, even about the most insignificant things. The first time I asked her name, she told me it was Cassie and that she was 15.

When Tom was in junior high he developed an interest in fire. He didn't just like to watch fire; he liked to play with it. Several times his cat caught mice, and Tom—with a few friends—built a small fire behind the garage and roasted the half-dead creatures. Tom thought it was funny; he called them his crispy critters.

Lying, stealing, cruelty, drug abuse, promiscuity, and running away are some of the common behaviors associated with conduct disorder. Let's look at each one.

LIAR, LIAR, PANTS ON FIRE

Aimee lied more than she told the truth. It wasn't something she even thought about very much. Sometimes it was to avoid trouble. Her teacher would ask her why her homework wasn't done, and Aimee would invent a story about a relative involved in a near-fatal car crash. Aimee, of course, had to babysit the woman's three young children while her husband stood vigil at the hospital bed, so there just hadn't been time to worry about American history.

Often, though, the lies served no purpose. Aimee's mother would ask her what she'd had for dinner at a friend's house, and Aimee would say chicken when in fact she'd had meat loaf.

As Aimee grew, so did her lies. She told her parents school was fine when she hadn't been to some of her classes in a month. She assured her boyfriend she was on the pill, and continued to have sex using no contraception.

Lying is a common behavior among kids with conduct disorder. Why does a kid lie?

First of all, let's make it clear that almost all teens lie to their parents at some point or other. Your daughter looks you straight in the eye and says, "We were at the movies," when she really spent the evening making out in her boyfriend's car.

But the lying I see among kids with conduct disorder is more pervasive and persistent. Often, as in Aimee's case, the falsehoods serve no apparent purpose.

Dr. Anna Freud described lying as a normal part of a child's growing up. She observed that children went through three distinct phases of lying during the course of development.

First, very young children tell innocent lies based on *wishful thinking.* "I got inside the TV and had lunch with Big Bird," a 3-year-old tells his mother. Dr. Freud recommended ignoring this type of lying; condemnation or punishment might make the child severely anxious.

In the second stage, as the child grows, he becomes a

fantasy liar in response to *frustration*. He tells lies about things that he wishes were true, such as, "We're going to ride on a plane to see Grandma and Grandpa."

Later, children lie to gain material *advantages*: to protect themselves from punishment, to escape criticism, and to make themselves look good. "I lost my lunch money; can I have five dollars?" "But I was home by midnight—I checked it on my watch!" "Yep, all the teachers say I'm doing a great job this semester."

Honestly now—do you ever lie to your children? Kids learn about honesty by experiencing it. Parents, of course, are their primary role models. Many parents tell what they consider to be well-meaning lies. "It won't hurt," the mother assures her anxious child as she leads him into the pediatrician's office for a booster shot. The kid soon finds out that Mom told a big fat lie. The shot did hurt—it hurt a lot!

Lying injures trust, whether it is parent lying to child or vice versa. I know adolescents can be merciless in their questions. You tell your daughter to wait to have sex until she's more mature, and she hits you with, "When did you first have sex? I bet it wasn't with Dad." Many mothers, stumped for a response to this one, will lie. Don't. Instead, tell your teenager that your sex life is private and that you'd rather not discuss it with her.

In truth, most parents occasionally do lie to their children. Nonetheless, most kids grow up reasonably honest. Why, therefore, do a few become persistent liars?

Results of some studies suggest that children whose parents openly reject them use lying as an underground way to express aggression, to "get even." These children have learned how to create havoc in the family through their lies, and this gives them a sense of control. In their minds, unconsciously, they're taking revenge on adults by whom they feel they've been mistreated.

Lying is a classic form of acting out. Many of the kids I see are habitual liars; deceiving people gives them a feeling of power. Quite often their habitual lying has reached a point where it confuses their perception of reality. The fabricated stories interfere with their thought processes and their ability to look at a situation logically.

If your child lies frequently, what can you do about it?

First, do not encourage him to lie about his feelings, no matter how negative those feelings may be. Some parents actually encourage lying in certain circumstances. For example, the parents of a ninth-grade girl in my program said they were upset about her chronic lies. At the same time, however, they urged her not to reveal to me that her father had a drinking problem.

Second, it's best to leave the fine art of interrogation to Perry Mason. Kids can't stand being trapped with questions that force them to choose between confessing and telling another lie. You know your child lied about her whereabouts yesterday. Don't be tempted to set a trap. The message you want to send her is that there is no need to lie—not that her lies aren't good enough and that she should try harder.

This isn't as difficult as it sounds. For instance, let's say she tells you she was doing homework at Susan's house yesterday evening but you know otherwise. Here are two possible reactions:

1. "Oh, is that so? Then why did Susan call here at nine-thirty last night and ask to talk to you? Do you take me for a fool? Who do you think you're trying to kid? How am I supposed to believe anything you say if you lie through your teeth like this?"

2. "Mmm-hmm. By the way, I saw Charlie's mom this morning and she said you and he seemed to have a really nice time at the movies last night. I just hope you manage to pull up that grade in algebra. I know you can if you work at it."

The second reaction, which is subtle and nonconfrontational, lets your daughter know that you recognize her dishonesty—but it doesn't accuse, berate, or demand a denial or an explanation from her. Also, it expresses love and concern. She will hear these messages and draw her own conclusions.

Third, and perhaps most important, try to understand the *meaning* of the lie instead of just dealing with the behavior itself. Did your daughter fib about where she went last night because you haven't given her any freedom to date? Did your 15-year-old son lie about the grades he's getting in English because his father would beat him if he found out?

Finally, if a punishment is in order, chose your method carefully. Though some parents err by failing to punish lying or other unwanted behavior, others mete out extraordinarily heavily punishments that do not fit the crime. Grounding, or taking away certain privileges, is appropriate. Beatings are not. A serious lecture about the value of owning up to our mistakes is appropriate. Screams, threats, sarcasm, and scorn are not. It's right to make a child feel guilty for lying about breaking your bedroom window—but it's wrong to make him feel he's the scum of the earth. A youngster who regularly feels that he's worthless and despised may eventually become bent on destroying himself.

STEALING

When you were a kid did you ever steal anything? If you were like most of us, there was probably at least one time when you pocketed a package of gum or candy while your mother was at the supermarket checkout counter.

I'll never forget my own early experiment with theft. I was about 4 years old. My mother took the whole family shopping for clothes. While she was busy looking in another department, I came across the most beautiful pair of cowboy boots I'd ever seen. They were just like the kind Ben Cartwright wore on *Bonanza*. When no one was looking, I took off my sneakers and stepped into those boots—never mind that they were meant for someone about Cartwright's size. Although I could barely walk without falling on my face, somehow I managed to get out into the parking lot and over to the car. It was there my mother found me. She carried me back into the store, boots and all, and made me confess my sin to the shoe department manager.

For most of us, once or twice is all it takes before we learn to curb our impulses and respect the property rights of others. A good share of kids with conduct disorder never learn this lesson.

Denny is typical of a kid with uncontrollable fingers. Even before he was old enough to go to school, he was always bringing home something that didn't belong to him—an apple from the fruit stand, nails from the hardware store, a toy from a playmate's house. Denny's parents always made him return the items, but that didn't seem to curb his urge to steal. At age 13, he was shoplifting records, tapes, and sports clothes and swiping money from his friends' bookbags and wallets.

I've said before that kids with conduct disorders have trouble controlling their impulses. Stealing is one manifestation of this lack of impulse control. Sure, I'd love to have my neighbor's Mercedes and you probably would, too. But we have built-in controls that say, "Wait a minute. Stop and think. Don't do it." The kid with conduct disorder doesn't have those controls.

Why we stop ourselves from stealing may be not high-minded moral principles, but simple fear of the consequences. As far as results go, it doesn't really matter.

I know that if I steal my neighbor's car, I'll be doing something basically wrong. Not only that, but I know I'll be in deep trouble with the neighbor and the police if I get caught.

But a kid like Denny can't see the consequences of his actions. Unlike others his age, he can't seem to put himself in the place of the victim. Kids with conduct disorder are extremely self-centered. They don't have what we might consider an ordinary, normal amount of empathy.

Finally, many of these kids have a poor self-image and

underdeveloped social skills. Many steal to compensate for dismal home lives. It's not uncommon to see a kid try to buy friendship with the stolen goods.

What should a parent do if a child is stealing? There are several steps you can take.

1. Acknowledge the problem. It doesn't matter how small the theft; you have a problem whether your son is continually stealing paint brushes from the school art room or jewelry and appliances from neighbors and local stores. Stealing gum and stealing cars is the same basic phenomenon.

2. Try to discuss the problem without yelling or threatening. Don't resort to name-calling. Explain in detail what constitutes stealing and why stealing is wrong. (Ideally, this kind of explanation should start very early in a child's life.)

3. Establish clear rules and penalties for stealing. Aside from returning the stolen object, the child should be made to pay for his mistake in another way. If he stole from a neighbor, he might clean the neighbor's garage or rake leaves for him.

4. Provide adequate supervision. Many kids who steal have too much time on their hands and do a lot of wandering about. Make it clear that the child should return home promptly after school. Regular room checks and even pocket checks—while distasteful to you—may be called for.

KIDS WHO HURT OTHERS

Jeff pushed a two-year-old neighbor boy into the deep end of a swimming pool and didn't even seem sorry when the baby's mother pulled him out, crying and choking.

Susan babysat for the money, but she didn't care about the kids. She'd put an 18-month-old to bed without changing his dirty diaper, and when he screamed she'd turn off his night light and close the door to his room so he wouldn't disturb her TV watching.

Nick knew his friend Matt had received twenty dollars from his grandmother as a birthday present, and he knew the envelope was in Matt's bedroom. When the two of them were at Matt's house watching TV, Nick went upstairs "to go to the bathroom." While he was up there, he found the envelope and pocketed the twenty-dollar bill.

Chet's mother once found him putting the cat in the freezer. He didn't even act ashamed or embarrassed. "Cats get hot," he said defensively.

Occasionally kids in their teens and early twenties—and some kids even younger—commit very serious crimes against other people and show no remorse when they're caught. They shrug their shoulders and act as though it's no big deal. In April 1989, the city of New York was shocked when a group of seven 13-to-15-year-old boys accosted a nighttime jogger in New York's Central Park, beat, raped, and sodomized her, and left her for dead. When arrested, they laughed and joked about the incident—which was just one of several assaults they had committed during an episode of "wilding."

The most disturbed and disturbing of conduct-disordered youngsters are the antisocial personalities or "psychopaths." People with antisocial personality have deeply entrenched problems in their ability to relate to the world. On an intellectual level they know right from wrong. But on an emotional level, they apparently couldn't care less.

Mercifully, not all antisocial personalities are violent. Some are con men, always in search of the perfect hustle, the most creative scheme for ripping people off. They're proud of their ability to outsmart everyone else, and unconcerned about the consequences. These are the ones who will suavely sell you the Brooklyn Bridge if you're ignorant enough to buy it.

But violent psychopaths can commit atrocious crimes. And what's so scary is that these kids initially may seem like the boy or girl next door—good-looking, polite, intelligent. They are often good actors whose performances can fool their parents, the police, psychiatrists, and, of course, their victims.

Not every kid who is violent is a psychopath. Mitch, for example, grew up in a home with no rules. His alcoholic father abused his mother. She, in turn, abused Mitch and his sister. At an early age Mitch learned not to hang around home. He took to the streets with his buddies, many of whom were kids like him. They were drinking beer well before their teen years, and soon they discovered how good drugs made them feel. One night they stole a car and drove around the city. Then someone proposed robbing an all-night grocery store. Armed with a knife, Mitch walked in with the others and ordered the store clerk to open the till. The man reached behind the counter to pull the alarm. In anger Mitch stabbed him, inflicting a slight wound in his arm. Then, horrified, he turned and ran.

A kid who is basically a psychopath probably won't get better. A kid like Mitch, with help, has a chance.

What are some of the warning signs of kids who seem headed toward a career of cold-hearted crime?

In his book *High Risk: Children Without a Conscience*, Dr. Ken Magid lists the following attributes of kids with severe character deficits:

1. Lack of ability to give and receive affection
2. Self-destructive behavior
3. Cruelty to pets and young children
4. Phoniness
5. Stealing, hoarding, and gorging
6. Speech problems
7. Extreme control problems
8. Lack of long-term childhood friends
9. Abnormalities in eye contact
10. Crazy lying
11. Preoccupation with blood, fire, and gore
12. Superficial attractiveness and friendliness with strangers
13. Learning disorders
14. Parents who seem unreasonably angry

A child with one or a combination of these attributes is at risk for the eventual development of antisocial personality.

It isn't so hard to see how the Mitches of the world become

violent. Exposed to violence in the home, with little parental supervision and an ego that has been kicked like a soccer ball, these kids can easily cross the line. It doesn't help if they come from a low-income family. Many children of poverty learn early to take what they want despite the risks.

What is more difficult is to understand how a personality can become truly antisocial. There may be a genetic component: It's known that antisocial parents are more likely than others to produce antisocial children. Couldn't this be a function of environment? Partly, perhaps, but not totally. In several studies, twins who were separated at birth from their antisocial parents and reared by normal parents still became antisocial at a higher-than-average rate.

THE BOND BETWEEN PARENT AND CHILD

Your newborn baby looks into your eyes and you smile. The baby cries and you pick her up in a soothing embrace. You walk the floor with her during the colic. All the cuddles and kisses, the smiles and gentle words serve to bond the two of you, to lay the foundation for your future relationship.

Sometimes an infant fails to bond. Infants who have spent their early weeks in institutions or in multiple foster homes are more likely to be unattached. But unattachment can also occur in a two-parent family. Typically these children are unwanted, neglected, and sometimes abused. Stiff and wooden, they do not babble and coo like normal babies. Not only is a baby without a bond more likely to wither physically, but something in the emotional makeup dies on the vine.

Kevin was an unattached child, the son of a confused, mentally unstable teenage girl who wasn't sure who had fathered her baby. Kevin spent the first three years of his life bouncing from one foster home to another. When he was 4, he was adopted by a family with three other adopted children. His mother told me that when they first saw Kevin they were totally charmed: "He sat on my lap and called me Mama. He cried at the end of the visit and said he wanted to stay with us. How could we refuse?"

The once happy household quickly disintegrated after Kevin arrived to stay. Even though the other children were older and bigger, he terrorized them. One time he pushed his older sister out the second-story window of their house and blamed it on the other brother. The child spent a month in traction. The next thing his mother knew, the family cat disappeared. Kevin swore he had seen the neighbor's dog with a cat in its mouth. Months later his mother surprised Kevin kneeling near the apartment dumpsters, strangling a cat. She screamed, and Kevin reluctantly let the animal go. It dawned on her that this might be how they had lost their pet, too.

Sad to say, many unattached kids like Kevin don't outgrow their antisocial behavior. Instead, as they grow older, they work on perfecting their techniques.

OPPOSITIONAL BEHAVIOR

Does your child often:
Lose his temper?
Argue with adults?
Defy or refuse adult requests or rules?
Deliberately do things to annoy people?
Blame others for his mistakes?
Become easily annoyed by others?
Become angry and resentful?
Show vindictive or spiteful behavior?
Swear or use obscene language?

This is called oppositional behavior. Most children with conduct disorder show most of these behaviors.

Some kids are given a diagnosis of oppositional defiant disorder. While they are hard to live with, they are considered *not* to have conduct disorder because they do not routinely violate the rights of others.

Sometimes the difference between the kid with a conduct

disorder and one with oppositional defiant disorder is a function of age. Younger kids usually don't have the opportunity to perform openly antisocial acts, so they internalize their actions.

RUNNING AWAY FROM HOME

Martha's parents watched their daughter with some other kids in treatment for conduct disorder and smiled sadly. "She looks so happy here," her mother said. "Why can't she be that way at home?"

Martha, at 14, had run away from home in the past year more times than her parents could count. Sometimes an argument would prompt her to walk out. More often than not her parents would come home to find Martha and a few favorite clothes gone.

They'd call every friend she had, comb the streets, stake out the school. But Martha knew how to stay hidden and she wouldn't climb out of her cocoon until she was good and ready. Usually that was within a week. Once she stayed gone for a month.

Running away is a common behavior associated with conduct disorder. While boys tend to be more aggressive and express their anger directly, girls with conduct disorder frequently choose less violent ways to vent their hostility. Running away is one way to do this.

Running away from home is a good way to make parents miserable and get back at them for anything they've done. Often the girl is immature and unstable. Usually there is a history of family discord.

Many of the kids I see in the program, however, run away for more practical reasons. They come from dysfunctional families and somewhere along the line they decide it is simpler to stay away. Sometimes they are running away from abusive parents. One girl currently in treatment at Laurel Oaks was being sexually abused by both her stepfather and her brother. By comparison, life on the streets didn't seem so bad, not even when she had to steal to survive.

SUICIDE—THE ULTIMATE DESPAIR

The following combination often proves lethal:

A conduct-disordered kid.
Depression.
Access to guns and other weapons
Access to drugs.
A history of aggressive behavior.

Toss those ingredients together and what you sometimes end up with is suicide.

Adolescent suicide had reached alarming proportions. About 5,000 teenagers in the United States take their own lives every year. That's about twelve kids every single day.

After all we've said about the harm that some kids with conduct disorder inflict upon others, it may be hard to believe that they are often their own worst victims. In fact, kids with conduct disorder are at particular risk for suicide.

Most people assume that it is the depressed teen who's more likely to kill himself. Depressed teens do, of course, commit suicide, but they are more likely to contemplate the act than to actually follow through. By contrast, the kid with conduct disorder is more inclined to pull the trigger or tighten the noose around his own throat. In one study of prisoners, 60 percent had attempted suicide at least once.

Many of the kids I treat not only have conduct disorder but also depression, a combination that makes the possibility of suicide even more real.

At 16, Zach had already had more dates in court than most kids have with the opposite sex. Arson, muggings, truancy, assault with a rifle, and destruction of property were some of the charges. Zach wore his bravado like cheap cologne. He was the best, the toughest, the coolest. A week before he was sentenced for assault, he hanged himself in the juvenile detention center.

Despite their bravado, many kids with conduct disorder actually suffer from low self-esteem. Many despise themselves. By nature, they are impulsive and aggressive. The result can be an explosion of violence directed inward.

PROMISCUITY

"It has about as much meaning as going to the bathroom. It's no big thing—just something to do."

That's Eve talking about sex. Eve's quite an expert, at least on the mechanics. This 15-year-old has already slept with about thirty-five different boys and men. She shakes her head when anyone asks her why, and admits she doesn't even particularly like sex.

Many kids with conduct disorder are promiscuous. In boys, this is often just one of several behavior problems. In girls, promiscuity may be the main symptom, closely associated with running away.

A great many kids today are sexually active, so just because your son or daughter is having sexual intercourse doesn't mean you're dealing with conduct disorder. Teenagers' emerging sexuality gives them new feelings of power and competence. They're eager to test this powerful force in their lives, and eager to prove to themselves that they measure up to other kids their age.

What makes some teens promiscuous? One study of suburban high school students found that the kids most likely to engage in early, indiscriminate sex came from unhappy families. A stable and loving family environment and college plans were the two factors that appeared to weigh heavily against promiscuity.

Like many conduct-disordered kids, the ones I see who are promiscuous tend to come from dysfunctional families. Often they have been the victims of abuse, either physical or sexual. Many have run away to escape poor family situations, only to find the streets as harsh as anything they left behind. Some discovered that sex was their ticket to survival on the street.

Kids learn by watching their parents. In some cases, parents talk one way and act quite differently. It's the old problem of the double standard.

Lily's mother was constantly repeating that men were useless and not to be trusted. Hadn't Lily's father run out on them when she was only 3? No money, no word, nothing for all these years. Stay away from boys, Lily. Study hard, make something of yourself. You don't need a man. Lily smiles when she recites her mother's litany to me but her eyes look dead. She long ago lost track of all the men who drifted through her mother's bedroom. Why, she wonders aloud, is everyone so upset at her just for doing what Mommy does?

Promiscuity is self-defeating behavior. It's a good way for a kid to show the world, and Mom and Dad, how angry, hurt, or lost she is. Her negative feelings aren't expressed in a violent manner. Instead, they're directed inward.

SUBSTANCE ABUSE

The vast majority of kids with conduct disorder are not strangers to drugs and alcohol.

Many are the children of parents who are themselves heavy drinkers or drug users. They may have grown up sneaking Dad's beer, or perhaps relatives actually encouraged them to drink because it looked so cute and grown-up.

Some kids are chronically agitated, anxious, or generally uncomfortable, and have learned to take a drink, smoke a joint, or pop a few pills to calm down. As we noted earlier, the professional term for this behavior is *self-medication*. These youngsters are trying to act as their own doctors, using what they can get their hands on to make themselves feel better.

Sometimes the anxious, uncomfortable feelings simply result from too much prior drug use, and go away when the kid enters a treatment program and becomes drug-free.

Other times the feelings are part of a treatable psychiatric condition, such as depression or attention deficit disorder with hyperactivity (ADDH). In these cases, the child may in fact need medication. However, the medication he needs isn't the stuff he's finding in the family liquor cabinet or on the street. At Laurel Oaks, we take questions of medication very seriously. We're well aware that correct diagnosis, prescription, and monitoring are critical parts of a serious treatment program.

To return to the issue of street drugs: It's obvious that drug use and behavior problems are intimately connected. One example is the child who steals to buy drugs. Another is the kid who skips days of school, preferring to spend the time getting high with friends.

Drugs—particularly cocaine and crack at the time of this writing—have been called the scourge of our society, the biggest threat facing this and future generations. They are, in effect, turning certain city streets into war zones and ruining untold lives. It's no wonder our nations's leaders, including President Bush, have declared war on drugs.

Alcohol and drug abuse. Why is it so widespread? What are some of the effects? Most importantly, what can we do about it? Let's make this our next topic.

Chapter 6

The Dual Diagnosis Dilemma: Drugs and Conduct Disorder

Drugs. It wasn't too long ago that drugs were something you worried about when your child reached adolescence. Today, you have to do without the luxury of time. Today, your fourth-grader is being confronted with someone trying to get him or her to "just try it." Unfortunately, too many kids who try it, like it. And, despite the "Just Say No" campaign, saying no isn't very easy for many teens and younger children.

The facts are hard to ignore:

- Ninety percent of all high school students have smoked marijuana at least once; 60 percent had their first experience between the sixth and ninth grades.
- In the past twelve years, drug-related suicides, accidents, and overdoses have steadily increased.
- Sons of alcoholic fathers are four to five times more likely to become alcoholics themselves than sons of nonalcoholic fathers.

You may be wondering why I would include a chapter on drugs in a book about conduct disorder. It's simply because, very often, the conduct-disordered kids I see are also heavy users of drugs and alcohol.

"Did the drugs make her steal, doctor?" Many parents are tempted to blame their child's unacceptable behavior on drug effects themselves. But this is actually a "Which came first, the chicken or the egg?" question. While certainly drugs and alcohol can serve to unleash aggression, spark impulsivity, and disinhibit even the most self-conscious kid, it's too simple always to explain away conduct disorder by blaming everything on drug or alcohol abuse.

Remember, conduct disorder is only a description of behavior: behavior that either impinges upon other people's rights or falls outside the boundaries of what society considers acceptable. While most kids with serious drug problems also are conduct-disordered, it doesn't follow that you can blame all behavior problems on substance abuse.

True, some therapists who specialize in treating alcohol and drug dependence see "addiction" as a package. They say the drug abuse is the first thing to treat; behavior improvement follows naturally. Frequently, they are right.

WHY DO SOME KIDS USE DRUGS AND ALCOHOL?

First of all, I want to go on record saying that I'm not a purist when it comes to chemical dependency. Dogmatists believe that every adolescent who uses drugs was born with an addiction just waiting to happen. But I don't buy that. I don't believe every kid who comes into my program using drugs—even if he uses heavily—was born an addict, is an addict, and always will be an addict.

Certainly, some of them *are* dependent on mood-altering chemicals. Some may be full-blown addicts. More often, though, their drug use is not so much a physical addiction as a way to try to fill an underlying emotional void. Typically, a young person's drug problem has developed in response to a variety of environmental and psychological factors. In other words, addressing *only* substance abuse may be missing the point. There are many reasons why a kid uses drugs. Here are a few:

1. A traumatic move to a new town. This results in feelings of loss and isolation. Joining the drug-use crowd is a way of gaining immediate acceptance.
2. Peer pressure. This explanation is sometimes a bit overplayed. Nonetheless, it's a real problem, since teenagers have a deep need to feel they fit in with kids their own age.
3. "Rebellion" against the establishment. This comes in many different forms, and is by no means always bad. Some kinds of rebellion are developmentally appropriate.
4. Simple enjoyment of the drug-induced high. This is the same reason many adults use alcohol and drugs. Unfortunately, the potential for becoming dependent on the chemical is rather high.
5. Parents who look the other way, or even encourage drinking or drug use in subtle ways.
6. A biological predisposition to use alcohol or drugs to excess. Not enough is known about the genetics of addictive behavior, but it's clear that alcoholism tends to run in families, and that young people who drink too much are also apt to use and abuse marijuana, cocaine, and other drugs.

Most people (but by no means all) eventually learn that they can't *permanently* snuff out pain or anxiety with alcohol or pills. But adolescents don't have the benefit of experience. For many of them—especially those troubled to begin with—drugs offer temporary but alluring relief from pain. A chemical high can give the illusion of control over that quintessential teenage dilemma: the struggle to cut the umbilical cord and yet maintain a caring relationship with Mom and Dad. Kids who stay drunk or high are able to avoid confronting their real fears and anxieties (it's worth noting that addiction can be described as a disease of avoiding feelings). Of course, they like the way the high feels. And if they drink or do drugs with friends, getting high is a social activity that reinforces a sense of belonging.

Let's look at some of the kids I see who use drugs and/or alcohol.

FAMILY TIES

Tim was 16 when I met him after he had been arrested half a dozen times for driving under the influence. Usually he was lucky, but the last accident had wrapped his father's car around a tree and landed his buddy in the hospital.

Drinking was no big deal in his house, Tim told me. Both his parents drank daily, though rarely to the point of excess. Wine was served at dinner, and from the age of 13 Tim was allowed a glass for himself. Tim's dad often rewarded good behavior with a beer. For example, Tim knew that if he helped his father mow the lawn, after the grass was cut they'd sit on the patio together and relax with a cold beer. A few times Tim had even talked his father into buying a case of beer for a party Tim and his friends were having.

Surprisingly, a lot of the parents I meet are not upset by their teenager's drinking. In fact, many are openly relieved that their son or daughter is drinking instead of doing drugs. It took a long time for Tim's parents to understand that by serving alcohol to their son and his friends liquor, they were both breaking the law and sending a mixed message.

"I'd rather have him drink at home," Tim's father said. But Tim saw his parents' sanction of his drinking as a blank check, a license to drink whenever and wherever he pleased.

HOW PARENTS ENCOURAGE SUBSTANCE ABUSE

"Enabling" is a form of behavior that supports or even encourages out-of-control drinking and drug use.

Here is one example of how it works:

Lindsay stayed out until three a.m. Her mother goes into her room to awaken her the next morning for school and catches the unmistakable odor of marijuana smoke from the pile of clothes left lying on the floor. She tries to get her daughter on her feet, but Lindsay is spaced out. She falls back onto the bed and sleeps for the rest of the day.

So her mother calls the school and says that Lindsay has the flu. The next day she writes a note asking the school to excuse the absence. This is what's known as family-related "enabling" behavior. Lindsay's mother is covering up for her. It may seem like a favor in the short run. But in the long run, the cover-up allows Lindsay to get away with her wild evening of drug abuse. It removes the natural consequence (which in this case would have been an unexcused absence from school and whatever penalty that entailed). It helps Lindsay avoid taking responsibility for what she does. And in subtle ways, despite any punishment that's involved, the cover-up encourages Lindsay to repeat her aberrant behavior.

Parents often contribute to their teen's problem—first, by refusing to believe what their eyes plainly see, and second, by making excuses.

Joy, a true alcoholic at the age of 17, had been drinking since she was 12. Her parents noticed that their liquor supply seemed to dwindle quickly. They also noticed that Joy spent a lot of time alone in her room and required an inordinate amount of sleep.

But excuses came easier than the truth. One day her mother walked into the bedroom after Joy had downed most of a fifth of vodka—before she'd had a chance to get rid of the bottle. Groggy and staggering, Joy admitted she'd had "a drink."

Her mother believed her. It wasn't until months later, when

the police brought Joy home after she'd passed out in a bar, that her parents had to admit she had a serious problem.

THE WARNING SIGNS

Do you think your teenager may be using drugs or alcohol? Has your normally dependable student suddenly started bringing home mediocre grades? Or perhaps your daughter, once a bubbly extrovert, has gradually turned evasive and secretive?

Read the following signs of substance abuse, and try to decide if the general picture applies to your adolescent:

1. Withdrawal from friends and family
2. Erratic and irritable behavior
3. Loss of appetite
4. Dilated pupils or red eyes
5. Neglect of activities that formerly brought pleasure
6. Inability to have fun
7. Few interest or hobbies
8. Hostile, dishonest, and manipulative relationships with others
9. Irresponsible behavior
10. Sniffling; runny nose
11. Unprovoked fits of yelling and screaming; treatment of parents or teachers as "the enemy"
12. Neglect of appearance
13. Change of friends
14. Memory impairment
15. Drop in grades; truancy
16. Chronic lying
17. Evidence of drugs or paraphernalia
18. Money or valuables missing from the house
19. The feeling that you've lost your child

Of course, these are general descriptions that may apply to a wide range of adolescent problems. Drug abuse, however, increases the likelihood that several or many of these descriptions will apply.

THE DRUGS KIDS LIKE TO TAKE

It's worth noting that alcohol and drug use go together. In your parent's day, and possibly even in your own high school years, alcohol was the only mood-altering chemical most kids could get their hands on. That changed in the late 1960s, when marijuana, LSD, and other drugs became popular. Nowadays, kids who drink almost invariably use other drugs, too.

What drugs are we talking about? These are the ones the kids in my program have used most often:

Marijuana: As you probably know, the kid high on marijuana typically acts mellow, laid back, and tired. (In a few people, however, it can cause excitement, agitation, or a false sense of stability.) Besides producing lethargy, marijuana interferes with the ability to concentrate. Conduct-disordered kids who use *only* marijuana are more likely to have problems with truancy than to commit violent crimes. They're the type who hang out in the woods smoking pot, not the type who rob old ladies at knifepoint. Paraphernalia you should look for includes roach clips, screens, and cigarette papers.

Cocaine or crack: Cocaine used to be so expensive that most teenagers couldn't afford to try it. In its smokable form, known as crack, however, cocaine is now becoming commonplace among teens. Crack is a powerful stimulant. The kid who smokes it becomes agitated and "wired." Cocaine in any form can increase impulsiveness, which is one of the hallmarks of conduct disorder. Even cocaine won't turn a wallflower into Jack the Ripper, but if a kid does have aggressive tendencies, this drug can trigger violence. Crack is highly addictive. Using it just a few times can cause severe withdrawal symptoms, including depression, paranoia, and lethargy. Telltale signs include sniffling, weight loss, and paranoia. Cocaine-related paraphernalia includes spoons, nasal inhalers, mirrors, baking soda, pipes, and the very small transparent plastic vials in which crack is sold.

Hallucinogens: Recently there has been a slight resurgence in the popularity of hallucinogenic drugs, such as LSD and "mushrooms" (peyote buttons, which naturally contain a hallucinogenic chemical). These mind-altering drugs interfere with perception. They can cause visual hallucinations (such as colorful paisley patterns superimposed on everyday objects), and they often make the user feel he has profound insight into the meaning of life. Kids on hallucinogens may laugh a lot and act giddy and silly, or they may go into a reverie, staring at the same object for endless minutes. They may also have a "bad trip" dominated by overpowering anxiety or paranoia.

Alcohol: Yes, alcohol is a drug, and it's the drug kids use most regularly and routinely. The only reason we don't always think of it that way is that in our society alcohol is a *legal* drug—at least for adults who aren't behind the wheel of a car.

Unlike adults, kids cheerfully admit that they drink to get drunk. At a teenage party where alcohol is served you're apt to find sloppy, falling-down-type behavior, loud slurred speech, and a general loss of control and decorum. After the initial euphoria, alcohol can cause depression or trigger violence.

All "recreational" drugs cause a loss of inhibitions. Thus, a kid who's inclined toward acting-out behavior will be even more inclined that way while under the influence. When you're high, you don't spend much time worrying about consequences.

Parents tend to go to extremes in their response to teenagers' alcohol and drug use—either overreacting or underreacting. The parent who cries, screams, swears, or beats his kid will certainly make an impression: that of an out-of-control grownup who loses his cool when things don't go his way. He's hardly an effective role model. On the other hand, the parent who grins, shrugs, looks the other way, or even buys the keg for the party will come across as a moral weakling—someone the kid can criticize, laugh at, and ultimately ignore. This type of parent quickly loses all leverage on his adolescent's behavior.

As a parent, you should realize that your teen will almost surely have the opportunity to experiment with alcohol and drugs sooner or later. Some degree of experimentation is normal and appropriate, but this behavior must still be dealt with firmly and clearly.

SELF-HELP GROUPS FOR ALCOHOL- AND DRUG-ABUSING TEENS

Many people sincerely believe that the best way to treat a kid with a drug or alcohol problem is just to get him into Alcoholics Anonymous (AA) or its more recent cousin, Narcotics Anonymous (NA). I only partly agree—but more about that in a minute. First, let's define our terms. What are these self-help programs, and how do they operate?

Briefly, the history of AA begins in 1935 with two alcoholics, a doctor and a stockbroker, who were at the end of their ropes. Both men had tried traditional medicine, religion, and various other ways to bring their lives under control—without results. It was through friendship and mutual support that they finally were able to stop drinking. When one felt like taking a drink, the other helped him get past the temptation. Both men believed the turning point had been accepting that they were powerless over alcohol, and that only a power greater than themselves—a "higher power"—could help them do without alcohol. Eventually they began helping other alcoholics get sober. From these simple beginnings grew an organization that now has millions of members in countries all over the world.

AA is a fellowship. It has no rigid rules, no fees, and a

minimum of organization, and its goal is personal sobriety, not wholesale reform of other people. Even though its principles refer to a "higher power," AA had no affiliation with any religion, and though it welcomes new members it does not evangelize or recruit.

Organizations that were inspired by AA include Al-Anon (alcoholic families helping other families with the same problems), Y.E.S. (Youth Enjoying Sobriety), Alateen (teenagers with alcoholic parents helping other teens in the same situation), Drugs Anonymous, Narcotics Anonymous, Nar'Anon Family Groups, Families Anonymous (parents helping one another deal with problem children), and others. It's easy to get information on local chapters of these groups right from the Yellow Pages of your phone book.

Atheists don't need to panic at the mention of God in the 12 steps! In AA, the concept of a "higher power" is interpreted very loosely. Kids who have absorbed religious training will probably understand their higher power to be God. Those who have had little exposure to religion, or who reject the idea of God, will still be able to relate to "group conscience," "the Higher Self," "Nature," or another term for something stronger and wiser than themselves.

The main reason why self-help groups such as AA flourish is that, for many people, they *work*. But although AA is an excellent program, it's mostly geared for grownups. NA is more focused on adolescents, and is frequently the group that adolescent drug abusers say they prefer. These support groups can make a crucial difference to kids with alcohol and drug problems—*but they're only one piece of the puzzle*. It's been my observation that, by themselves, the support groups don't always respond fully to kids' special needs or deal with the depth of their problem.

True, some youngsters do very well in AA and NA: they get off alcohol or drugs and they stay off. Interestingly, it's often the antisocial kids who seem to thrive on these programs. Perhaps it's because they find they can't con the members with their usual lies and excuses. Others in the

Here are the "12 steps" that serve as AA's prescription for personal recovery. Although they speak in terms of alcohol, they are valid for dependency on drugs, too:

The 12 Steps of AA

1. We admitted we were powerless over alcohol—that our lives had become unmanageable.
2. Came to believe that a Power greater than ourselves could restore us to sanity.
3. Made a decision to turn our will and our lives to the care of God as we understood Him.
4. Made a searching and fearless moral inventory of ourselves.
5. Admitted to God, to ourselves, and to another human being the exact nature of our wrongs.
6. Were entirely ready to have God remove all these defects of character.
7. Humbly asked Him to remove our shortcomings.
8. Made a list of all persons we had harmed, and became willing to make amends to them all.
9. Made direct amends to such people wherever possible, except when to do so would injure them or others.
10. Continued to take personal inventory and when we were wrong promptly admitted it.
11. Sought through prayer and meditation to improve our conscious contact with God as we understood Him, praying only for knowledge of His will for us and the power to carry that out.
12. Having had a spiritual awakening as the result of these steps, we tried to carry this message to alcoholics, and to practice these principles in all our affairs.

---

group are con artists, too. They know too much to be fooled by a kid.

One problem with relying exclusively on an AA-type support group for teen therapy is that the program tries to change behavior without understanding *why* the behavior is occurring. That may work fine for adults. But most conduct-disordered kids are still dependent on their parents for support. Even if their family situation is full of negatives, they can't just walk away from home. In addition to exploring their inner selves, they need a personal advocate who can help them redefine their relationship with their parents and other authority figures. In short, adolescent "addicts" don't exist in a vacuum. AA and NA have a great deal to offer, but for most kids with conduct disorder they should be only one part of a comprehensive treatment plan.

A TENTATIVE SUCCESS

Many of the kids I see are like Allie. She had been abusing drugs off and on for five years when her parents brought her to my program. She hadn't been to school for six months, was routinely stealing money from her family, and would disappear for days and sometimes even weeks at a time.

Allie would stay at an older boyfriend's apartment, spending the day watching TV, getting high, and having sex whenever the boyfriend wanted it. Sometimes the sex got violent, and Allie got hurt and scared. Then she'd move to someone else's place for a while. Twice she got pregnant and her parents paid for abortions. They shouted, threatened, cajoled, bribed—but nothing seemed to change her behavior. Allie ignored them, and deepened her involvement with cocaine—then heroin.

Eventually she and a boyfriend were arrested for possession and sale of drugs, and spent some time in jail. Allie went into such severe withdrawal that she had to be hospitalized. A few days later she tried to commit suicide. At the Laurel

Oaks program, through a combination of individual therapy and small group sessions with kids her own age, Allie began to take a look at her behavior and what it was costing her and her family. In addition, she joined Narcotics Anonymous and her family joined Nar'Anon, a support group that helps family members see the role they are playing in this devastating family illness.

Now, a few months later, Allie is home and back in school. She admits school is tough. She'll see a "druggy" friend from the old days, or catch a whiff of marijuana in the lavatory, and for a moment she'll be almost overcome by the urge to give in and get high just one more time.

So far, something stronger has allowed Allie to stay on course. When I saw her yesterday, she smiled and said she was optimistic about the future.

Chapter 7

School and Conduct Disorder

"I could make $150 a week frying hamburgers. Who needed school?"

—High school dropout

Who needs school? That's a sentiment frequently expressed by the conduct-disordered kids I see. For many of them, school is simply a place to act out their inner conflicts. Some have been characterized as disruptive in class since almost the first day of kindergarten. Some have been hostile or even overtly aggressive toward teachers. Some have purposely destroyed school property. Many are truants, preferring to spend the day doing anything but going to school. Ultimately many of these kids become society's dropouts, whose work options are limited to minimum-wage jobs. This, in turn, leads to more frustration and to lower self-esteem.

After the family, the two factors with the biggest impact on adolescents are peer relationships and school. Let's look at the role of school in conduct disorder.

KIDS MOST TEACHERS HATE TO HAVE IN CLASS

Ronnie is every teacher's nightmare. Loud and disruptive, this 15-year-old is two hundred pounds of malice. He's verbally abusive to his teachers, and not shy about issuing threats. One teacher made the mistake of keeping Ronnie after school when he failed to turn in a homework assignment. The next day she found her tires slashed. Although she could never prove it, Ronnie's triumphant smile left no doubt in her mind who was responsible. Twice Ronnie had been suspended from school: once when a knife was found in his locker during a check, and again when he was seen spray-painting obscenities on the outside of the building.

Across the nation, there has been an unprecedented rise in the incidence of violence against school personnel and abuse of school property. Some classrooms have become battle-fields. It's not uncommon today to find schools manned by security patrols to ensure student and teacher safety.

Every school has its share of kids like Ronnie—hard on property, aggressive toward fellow students, contemptuous and sometimes menacing toward teachers. They are the kids who seem to spend class time doing little more than occupying a desk. Many are involved with drugs. Stealing, cheating, and lying are typical behaviors.

Then there are kids like Jack. This 13-year-old wouldn't hurt a fly. On the contrary, he's like an overly friendly puppy that makes a nuisance of itself. One of six children, Jack will do anything for attention even if it means humiliating himself. Unable to concentrate on schoolwork or sit still long enough to complete an assignment, he spends his school hours concocting elaborate jokes or dreaming of being a rock star, center stage, with everyone's attention focused on him. Sometimes Jack steals from his parents and pilfers drugs from his older brothers. He uses the loot to try and buy friends. But to the other kids Jack is a joke, the class dummy. So at a time in his development when friends are more important than ever, Jack spends much of his time alone inside himself.

Tricia is another type of kid who is having trouble in school. All through elementary school and junior high, she was an A student. Then her family moved to a neighboring town just before she was to start high school. Seemingly overnight, something changed. Her parents noticed that she rarely brought assignments home, even though she was taking some difficult courses. At school, her teachers found her indifferent to her studies. She no longer volunteered information in class. Nor did she seem to have any social life. When report cards were issued, Tricia's parents were shocked into realizing their daughter had a problem. She was failing half her subjects.

THE IMPORTANCE OF FRIENDS

According to one study on school disturbances, probably the best single factor that determines whether a kid has a significant behavior problem is how well he or she is liked by classmates.

Many kids with conduct disorder have few friends at school or none at all. This may be because they are bullies, physically or verbally threatening. These kids are often belligerent, too competitive, and given to fits of aggression when they lose. It shouldn't come as a surprise that most of the other kids prefer to stay clear of them.

Or they may be like Jack. Hungry for any type of attention, they disrupt the class with practical jokes and clowning. This initially amuses their peers, but eventually produces anger and dislike. They're seen as silly, immature, and unable to control themselves. Although they may have friends, there is no depth to the relationships, and they aren't able to maintain friendships over time.

Kids who are having problems in school because of depression or anxiety also are more likely to lack the support of friends because, in their despair, they don't have the energy it takes to cultivate friendships. An overly shy or withdrawn teenager sends out signals: Leave me alone. I'm untouchable.

Of course, not all kids with conduct disorder are friendless. As we said earlier in this book, a kid with conduct disorder need not be a loner, and may well be clever and unusually charming.

Some kids hang out with other troubled teens. In the case of a youngster with an aggressive conduct disorder, the group is apt to be a gang of similarly aggressive friends. The various types of antisocial or illegal activity the kids engage in are the social glue that holds the group together.

The other side of the coin is the nonaggressive kid with conduct disorder, who skips school to hang out doing drugs with like-minded friends—one environment in which he doesn't fell inadequate.

The need to belong, to find a comfortable spot for oneself, is never so acute as in adolescence. It is during these critical years that a young person is most vulnerable to this powerful and potentially destructive need to fit in with a group. An adolescent without friends travels a lonely road filled with dangerous twists and turns. On the other hand, having the *wrong* friends can be like traveling down a mountain in a car without brakes.

POOR ACADEMIC PERFORMANCE

"He's a bright boy with a high I.Q., but he doesn't live up to his potential."

I can't count the times I've heard parents of my patients describe their kid in these terms. And many of these parents are right. Not all conduct-disordered kids have above-average intelligence, but many do. Many are also clever and cunning.

Yet these same kids are flunking out of school. Why?

There are various reasons why kids with conduct disorder tend to do poorly in school. Let's look at some of them.

Neurological problems: As we discussed in prior chapters, conduct disorder is frequently found in kids with other problems, such as attention-deficit disorder, depression, or a learning disability. Although many of these disorders can be treated, they frequently go undiagnosed for many years or even indefinitely. A kid with a serious degree of hyperactivity, for example, could have an IQ rivaling that of an Oxford scholar, yet still be unable to perform in school because of his inability to sit still and concentrate. It's important to understand that intelligence and academic performance do *not* necessarily go hand-in-hand.

Low self-esteem: Many kids with conduct disorder have never had a success in school. Let's look at Neil. By the time he was in second grade, it was clear that Neil was going to have a hard time. He was bright, observant, and a good talker, but he just couldn't get the hang of reading. Though he tried his best, his papers looked like the work of a kindergarten kid, and it was all too easy to assume he took no interest or pride in what he was doing. Both his parents and the teachers blamed his poor academic performance on laziness, when in fact Neil had a learning disability. The other kids laughed at him when he stumbled over oral reading assignments, and taunted him at the playground when the teacher's back was turned. Neil grew up thinking his brain power was nothing to brag about. Since he was stupid, why try to learn? Instead, he spent his time getting into trouble. One day when Neil was 15, he walked out of school and decided he had had it. From then on he refused to go back.

Lack of motivation: Initially it doesn't seem to make sense that so many conduct-disordered kids are very bright, yet do poorly in school. But there is an explanation. No matter how intelligent a person is, if he isn't motivated to accomplish anything, he won't. Academic success depends upon more than raw materials. It takes motivation to succeed. Something has to make an adolescent want to get out of bed in the morning. Something has to propel him or her through the door and into the classroom. Something has to make him want to open up his mind in class and absorb what the teacher is saying.

To be a success in school, you have to pay attention and want to get good grades. But for conduct-disordered kids, grades are not enough reinforcement. For one reason or another—depression, unhappiness at home, fidgetiness, trouble concentrating, a history of failure in school—the kids I see are not motivated academically. It's no surprise that many of them become...

TRUANT

Kathy's parents both work and they leave the house before she wakes up, so it's up to her to get herself off in the morning. But lately Kathy hasn't felt much like getting out of bed. She's been out of school for three weeks, spending most of her days alone in her room.

Business is booming for Rich. His business is dealing crack, and at his high school, he's the man to find if you want to get high. He spends five days a week on the job. But even though his is an on-campus operation, Rich rarely finds the time or the desire to sit in on a class.

Maureen never liked school. It's too boring. The teachers are just glorified babysitters. What good does it do anyone to know whose side our country fought on in World War I? That's not cool. What's cool is spending the day with friends. Some days the gang goes into the woods to drink and get high until dinnertime. Other days they pair off and lose themselves in an afternoon of sex.

Three kids; three reasons for skipping school.

Among the kids I see, truancy is one of the most prevalent behavior problems.

Again, motivation is missing. Let's face it, school can be a tough place. Making it in that environment requires a lot of time and effort, not only from the kid himself but from the family. Often, with both Mom and Dad working, caught up in the daily struggle for economic advancement or survival, parents are not as involved in their teenager's life as they should be. For reasons that frequently are unclear, school is not the place where these kids get their strokes.

Then, too, these kids tend to live for today. They can't see what good school is doing them *now*. For a kid who hates school and is consistently reminded of her academic inferiority, the lure of freedom in the world outside may be too powerful to resist.

QUITTING FOR GOOD

Chronic truancy means falling hopelessly behind in everything. The end of the line is dropping out. Many conduct-disordered kids simply decide one day to turn in their books. They've decided they have bigger fish to fry.

Today, in central Florida where I work, the bigger "fish" is often dangled in their faces in the form of an unskilled job. Unemployment in this area is currently low, and entry-level jobs are begging for applicants. To a kid from a financially strapped family, the prospect of $150 a week seems too good to pass up. Remember, these kids are impulsive. They tend to dive before they've tested the water.

For most of them, the glamour of washing cars or working behind a fast-food counter soon wears off. Before long they realize that $150 a week doesn't pay many bills. With this realization comes despair. The question is, What am I going to do now?

Some kids with conduct disorder resort to stealing or drug dealing. Many simply give up and get more deeply involved with drinking and drug use. The lucky ones get professional help, and eventually find their way back to school.

In this half of the book we've talked about conduct disorder and its associated behaviors.

We've seen how to detect it's early signs, and how to recognize symptoms of other disorders that may or may not occur in conjunction with conduct disorder.

We've talked about normal adolescent development, and how to tell whether your teenager is simply going though a difficult adolescence or has more deeply entrenched problems causing his undesirable behavior.

Now, let's talk about some concrete things you can do to help your troubled teen.

PART II

Helping Teens with Conduct Disorders

Chapter 8

What Can the Family Do?

When was the last time you enjoyed your teenager? I don't mean tolerated—I mean actually got a kick out of being your kid's parent.

For many of you reading this book, the answer may be, "I don't remember when," or "When she was little."

I won't argue that being the parent of an adolescent is difficult, especially when the kid has a conduct disorder. Teenagers can be a pain in the neck. But for the parent who *appreciates* this difficult process we call adolescence, the teenager can also be a source of delight and a challenge to which the parent feels compelled to rise.

If you are simply going through the mechanics of being a parent—that is, if you are living under the same roof, putting food on the table, and saying "no" when you think you're supposed to—you are missing out on an emotional commitment to parenting. Your teenager will sense that you're not enjoying him and appreciating the qualities that make him unique.

Being the parent of a teenager is like playing cops and

robbers. You can just chase after your adolescent, which will often lead you down a blind alley. Or you can study the situation, try to understand the child's motivation, and get to the bottom of his behavior.

Most parents *want* to be good parents. Many, however, don't know how, often because they don't understand the adolescent process. Also, the day-to-day struggle to make a living saps the energy of many parents. They come home emotionally frazzled, with no energy left to expend on a troubled teen.

Finally, as a parent you should be aware that watching your son or daughter in the throes of adolescence may stir up some of your deepest feelings, not all of them positive.

For example, Sylvia had spent the past eight years of her sixteen-year marriage with a man who rarely spoke unless it was to ask her to pass the potatoes. As for their sex life, that was no more than a memory. Approaching 40, Sylvia felt old, fat, and unloved. At the same time, her daughter was blooming. Patty had started dating, and the boys swarmed around their house like bees around a hive.

Sylvia found fault with every boy Patty dated. When Patty came home five minutes past her curfew, her mother grounded her for a month. By this time the tension between mother and daughter was palpable. Patty began sneaking out and staying away until morning. When she was 16, she got pregnant.

It took a long time for Sylvia to admit that she was jealous of her daughter's youth and beauty. Only then could she and Patty begin to repair the relationship that had crumbled.

SOME PARENTING TOOLS

Only in recent years has psychiatry paid much attention to parenting and its role in conduct disorder. Today we know that it's possible to identify young children who may be prone to developing conduct disorder in adolescence. Once they've

been identified, their parents can be taught certain skills that
may help alleviate undesirable behavior. The goal, of course,
is to nip a potential conduct disorder in the bud.

Many of these parenting techniques are geared for young
children, and since most of you reading this probably have
adolescents, I won't get into too much detail here. However, I do
think it's useful for you to see some of the principles involved.

YOUR ATTENTION, PLEASE

Research has shown that the parents of aggressive children
are likely to respond in a positive way to the child's negative
behavior, and ignore or respond negatively to normal behavior.

With this in mind, some therapists teach parents of aggressive children the "attention rule." This is simply that a child
will work for attention, whether the attention is positive or
negative. Throwing tantrums, swearing, whining, and sulking
are all ways for kids to get a parent's attention. But the
attention then reinforces the bad behavior. Parents of children who throw tantrums are given this advice:

1. Look away from the child.
2. Move away from the child.
3. Maintain a neutral facial expression.
4. Don't speak to the child.
5. Continue ignoring the child until the tantrum ends.
6. Ignore the misbehavior every time it occurs.

REINFORCING GOOD BEHAVIOR

For some reason, parents of conduct-disordered children
tend to be more negative, critical, and rejecting than those of
"normal" kids. Moreover, these parents tend not to praise
their children. The lack of praise combined with criticism and
rejection works against the child's developing self-esteem.

Here are some rules of social reinforcement:

1. Be specific about what you are praising. For instance, "I like the way you share your toys."
2. Establish eye contact, smile, and move close to the child.
3. Be sincere and enthusiastic in your praise.
4. Praise immediately following the behavior you like.
5. Combine the praise with a kiss or hug.
6. Don't wait for the behavior to be perfect.
7. Praise in front of others.
8. Consistently praise the child, especially when he is learning a new behavior.

HOW TO AVOID AN IMPASSE

"Listen, young man. You live in my house, and you'll do as I say!"

That was Matt's father talking. In response, Matt stomped up the stairs to his room, locked the door and refused to go to school. Three days later he ran away from home.

All this over a shirt Matt wanted to wear to school.

Let's look at what happened, how it was handled, and how it might better have been resolved.

Matt is a 15-year-old who fancies himself the next Alice Cooper. Remember him? He was the rock star who used to perform with snakes wrapped around his neck and blow up his guitar at the end of the show. Lately, Matt had taken to wearing gruesome T-shirts depicting blood and guts, violence and horror—the kind of shirts inspired by heavy metal rock groups.

One day Matt made the mistake of appearing at the breakfast table before his father left for work. His father took one look at his son's shirt and did a double take. "You wear what I tell you until you're eighteen, or you can get out of the house. Now get up those stairs and put on something respectable."

Humiliated and feeling like a baby, Matt stewed and fumed and finally decided to run away. It was the only way he could see to maintain any control or dignity.

There was a better way to handle the above scenario. Matt might still be home if it had been used.

Very simply, Matt's father could have used the offensive T-shirt to initiate a discussion. It's important to understand that the discussion would not be over whether the shirt was in poor taste. Obviously, Matt thought the shirt was fine and his father thought it revolting. They could argue that point until they were both blue in the face, and nothing would be resolved. Rather, the discussion could revolve around whether it was within Matt's rights to wear such a shirt.

I had a similar incident with several kids in my treatment program. I invited them to do some research, and they ended up calling the American Civil Liberties Union to find out about individual rights. They learned about some cases that had reached the courts, and they reported all this back to me.

The important element here is the process itself, not specifically whether it's within Matt's rights to wear a shirt. The bottom line is that the kids in my program learned something, and tension was decreased. Parents sometimes make the mistake of getting too caught up in a specific behavior, and not involved enough in the process.

Matt's shirt wasn't going to hurt anyone. But he was making a fashion statement that was contrary to his father's taste. I'm not suggesting that the parent always has to give in. Boundaries have to be set, compromises made. Thus, Matt learns that his parents will tolerate one shirt but not the other. More important, he's allowed to experience the development of a sense of self.

For many parents, acknowledging when they've made a mistake is one of the hardest things in the world. I believe, however, that the ability to admit you are wrong is crucial in the parent/child relationship—especially in adolescence. There is no dishonor in backing down. All you need to say is, "I don't like it, but it's your choice." This is perfectly appropriate parental behavior. It doesn't control, but it allows your child to register in his mind that you disapprove of what he's doing. You're teaching him your values, but you're not forcing them down his throat. He'll get the message. Some day, when he wants to make a good impression on a job interview, he'll remember what you consider "appropriate" clothing, and he'll dress himself accordingly.

LABELING

If someone in authority has been telling you all your life that you're wonderful, intelligent, warm, funny, and sensitive, pretty soon you're going to believe those things about yourself and assume those qualities.

But if instead someone has called you stupid, mean, cold, and uncaring, eventually you will take on these characteristics.

The above is a thumbnail sketch of the *theory of attribution*. A prime example of how it works was a study done years ago. Social psychologists visited two schools: one in an upper-middle-class suburb, and the other in the inner city.

At the pristine suburban school, the psychologists told a classroom of students their room was filthy and disgusting (when actually it was a model of cleanliness). Lo and behold, the children in that classroom became more careless and sloppy. At the ghetto school, by contrast, the researchers praised students for their cleanliness and organization. Almost overnight, these kids took more interest and pride in keeping their classroom clean and running efficiently.

The theory of attribution says that if someone in authority attributes a quality to you, you begin to assume that quality. Kids with conduct disorder have rarely heard important people say positive things about them. Parents have often been critical. Peers have called them names. Teachers have thrown up their hands in disgust. In some cases, police officers have muttered about their desire to rid society of a "no-good kid."

It shouldn't come as any surprise that the kids have learned to act the part.

Let's look at how, in the course of therapy, an attribute that has always been seen in a negative way can be refocused in a positive light.

Jordan is a crack dealer. Believe me, this kid is no angel. He has stolen from his parents and sold drugs on the playground of an elementary school. But he has a strict code of ethics when it comes to "narking" (squealing) on his peers. He's resolved never, ever to turn a buddy in.

I see this as a very positive attribute. True, Jordan is using it in the context of criminal activity. But clearly he has a sense of right and wrong. The trick is to help him see the paradox in his actions. On one hand, he's hurting people by selling them drugs; on the other, he's protecting people by not narking. How can he reconcile the contradiction?

Pointing out contradictions is a large part of what therapy is all about. In a program such as we have at Laurel Oaks, teaching Jordan that drug-selling is harmful, illegal, and immoral is less than half the battle. The positive side of the issue—and the one we take pains to emphasize—is that Jordan has a core of loyalty, faithfulness, and goodness. Jordan needs to gain a wider perspective on life, so he can take that core quality and put it to some constructive, socially acceptable, *legal* use. Society is full of genuine opportunities for a kid with energy and loyalty: Jordan could succeed brilliantly in student government, advertising, or sales. He needs to be shown the long-term advantages of leaving the drug underworld and joining "legitimate" society.

BUILDING CLOSENESS

Some people call it bonding. But I don't think you need such a fancy word for spending time with your adolescent.

These days it's especially difficult. Both parents may work and the family is scattered, one here, one there, with little to bring them together at the end of the day or on weekends. Where does the time go? If you are going to spend time together, you have to make an effort. It's not going to happen magically, without motivation and planning.

1. Have dinner together. This may sound like a scene from *Ozzie and Harriet*, but I truly believe that the old-fashioned image of the whole family gathered around the dinner table at least several nights a week is a goal worth working toward. Turn the television and radio off and forget the newspaper. Try to focus on your children. What kind of day did they have? What was good and what was bad?

2. Try to spend a designated time each week with each child. There's nothing that says you have to do everything as a family. It's important that each child get some individual attention from Mom and Dad, because this encourages them to develop their individual qualities.

3. Let your teenager know that you too were young once. It's important that the parents of a teenager try to remember what it was like, the highs and lows, the first kiss, the pain of loving someone who didn't even know you were alive. Often a teenager who feels caught on the horns of a dilemma takes comfort from knowing that one of her parents went through the same thing.

For example, Lauren's boyfriend is pressuring her to have sex. Lauren is torn and her mother senses the problem. She relates her own confusing feelings about sex when she was a teenager. She's not indiscriminately passing on information such as, "Oh yes, I slept with ten boys when I was in high school." Instead, she's *selectively* relating her own emotional confusion. In essence she's saying, "I once felt as you do, and this is how I made my decision. Here's what went right—and here are some things that went wrong."

LEARNING TO TRUST

The kids in my program, both individually and with their families, participate in an exercise called Escape to Reality. This is basically an obstacle course that encourages every kid to strive for successful completion. It includes several impressive physical challenges, including a short but scary jump off a high platform to a trapeze. Safety precautions are observed, yet the trapeze jump is a heart-stopper for most people. Getting up the nerve to make the jump is an exercise in personal discipline and self-control. People who make the jump are thrilled at their success—they actually get an adrenaline rush that suffuses them with well-being and a sense of power. This is a potent reinforcement to whatever psychotherapy they're receiving. It's concrete proof that determination and follow-through *do* make a difference.

One of the central components of the Escape to Reality course is a thirty-foot-high wall. Every kid in the program is given the opportunity to try and scale the wall. If this sounds dangerous, let me reassure you that no one has ever been injured beyond a few cuts and bruises. Anyone who climbs the wall is spotted or, to use the mountaineering term, *belayed* by someone on the ground who holds the ropes that will prevent him from plummeting if he slips.

Belaying sounds easy, but it's an important task because it requires the trust of the climber. For some kids in the program, belaying a climber may be their first opportunity—ever—to let someone depend on them. The emotional impact of this exercise is high, and the psychological benefits are sometimes remarkable. Roger, an overweight, depressed boy with low self-esteem, tried to avoid belaying because he was certain he didn't have the coordination or muscle power to keep anyone from falling. Finally one day he reluctantly agreed to belay a much bigger kid. He was frightened, and the other boy was nervous. But Roger did the job and got him safely over the top. Afterward, he was visibly elated. From that day on he took the treatment program seriously, and eventually he developed a measure of the self-confidence he so desperately needed.

Although it may be hard for the uninitiated to understand how an obstacle course can provide a lesson in trust, think about it. If you're going to climb a high wall, don't you want to know that those holding the ropes—your only protection from slamming into the ground if you slip—will do their job? In most cases, conduct-disordered kids have not learned to trust others. Moreover, their family members have forgotten, or never knew, how to trust one another. But when they're faced with the wall, and they have to decide both who will scale it and who will belay, feelings surface like cream in a milk bottle. Does a father care enough about his son to belay him? Will a daughter who says she hates her mother really allow the mother to plunge to the earth if she loses her footing? Who is willing to trust whom, and to what extent?

After the exercise, the family and a therapist discuss what took place and the feelings that arose. Typically, conduct-disordered kids are not comfortable talking about their feelings, so this part is especially critical.

The important thing to remember about trust is that it has less to do with concrete events, and more to do with allowing yourself to get close to someone and express your feelings.

DISCIPLINE

"The kid doesn't need therapy. What he needs is a good swift kick in the rear."

That's Greg's dad explaining to me why treatment would be wasted on his son. As I pointed out to him, Greg has had more kicks in the rear than he can count. And he's still stealing and getting into trouble.

If force was a solution to conduct disorder, one would assume that all the sons and daughters of aggressive and controlling fathers like Greg's would toe the line.

Hitting a kid doesn't work. Never mind that many kids are too big and too threatening for a parent to lay a hand on. Some of them, given the opportunity, wouldn't mind leveling Mom or Dad.

Aside from the abuse implications of physical punishment, the parent who hits his or her child sends two messages.

First, there's the message that it's all right to be physically aggressive. To a kid who may be prone to aggressive behavior anyway, this has the effect of a spring tonic.

Second, there's the message that a quick slap evens the score. Hitting the kid for sticking his hand in the cookie jar in essence pays him back for his bad behavior. The slate is clean until the next time. This is counterproductive, because it removes an opportunity to make the youngster feel guilt—an often devalued emotion, but one that's important.

THE POWER OF GUILT

Guilt? Since when does a psychiatrist advise parents to make their kids feel guilty?

Personally, I think guilt has gotten a bad rap. Of course it's possible for a child who constantly feels guilty to become nervous and jittery. But conduct-disordered kids generally suffer from too *little* guilt, not too much. The kid who got hit for swiping a cookie doesn't learn anything—except that next time he'd better be quicker.

My gut feeling is that there's nothing like a little guilt for keeping a kid in line! How can you develop a conscience without guilt? It's impossible. A kid who truly does not feel guilt when he or she does something wrong is a kid without a conscience—a psychopath.

When a child is around 4, 5, or 6 years old, he starts to develop a conscience based on two related dynamics: wanting to please his parents, and being made to feel uncomfortable, i.e., guilty, when he does something that displeases them.

Let's take the cookie jar example again. If Jane is caught with her hand in the jar between meals, ideally the motivation not to repeat that behavior comes from the disapproving look on her mother's face. That look says, You've done something wrong and I'm disappointed in you. A slap on the hand may sting the nerve endings for a few seconds. But the guilt over knowing you've done something wrong, something that disappointed your parents, is an internal sore that's slower to heal. Wanting to avoid further guilt becomes the motivation for not repeating the incident.

PUNISHMENT TO FIT THE CRIME

The best punishments are connected to the crime.

Let's look at punishment. One of the most common punishments is restriction or "grounding." Sheila is caught stealing money from her mother's purse, and her mother's solution is to keep her from seeing her friends for a couple of weeks. All this does is make Sheila mad. It serves no real purpose other than to interfere with socialization, which is important at this stage of her life.

It would be to her parents' advantage to find a more creative way of dealing with the problem. For instance, they might find a book about stealing and make reading it a family event. The family would discuss it. The parents would tell Sheila how disappointed they were. Perhaps they would take away something she loved for a limited time such as use of the car, her stereo, or the telephone. This three-pronged punishment would thus include education, guilt, and "payment" by forfeiting something valuable.

When Henry, a 13-year-old, branded the carpeting in his father's new BMW with the car's cigarette lighter and then blamed it on his little sister, his father was ready to break his neck. But after talking about it, we came up with a more productive punishment. Henry was told he had to write an essay detailing what he had done wrong. This got him thinking about his actions. In addition, Henry had to contribute most of the money he had been saving for a new bike toward the repair of the carpeting in the car. The final part of his punishment was a brand-new job: washing the car twice a week, for pay, with the money he earned going toward the repair.

Incidentally, studies have shown that one of the best punishments for conduct-disordered kids is work detail, whether it's cleaning the bathroom, scrubbing floors, straightening out the garage, or weeding the flower beds.

MAKING YOUR EXPECTATIONS CLEAR

Before kids can live by the rules, they have to know the rules.

Many parents make the mistake of assuming their kids knows what's acceptable and what isn't. This isn't always true, especially in homes where rules are inconsistent and punishment is haphazard.

It's important that Johnny know exactly what you will tolerate and what you will not. Some people post the house rules—and the punishments for breaking them. If it says on the refrigerator that the penalty for arriving home ten minutes past curfew is to mow the lawn, then the kid knows the consequences up front. This defuses the confrontation that otherwise would occur when Johnny stepped over the threshold a half-hour past his curfew.

YOU'RE NOT ALONE

You say you've tried and still you can't get through. It's like beating your head against a brick wall: something's bound to give and it's not going to be the wall.

A parent, no matter how dedicated, cannot do it all. Sometimes help can come from others—a concerned teacher, an older person the troubled teen admires, someone willing to go out on a limb with the offer of a job. Let's now examine some possible sources of help.

Chapter 9

Solutions Outside the Home

A coveted spot on the high school basketball team, A teacher whose zest for learning is contagious. A beloved uncle who has ample time and isn't judgmental. Or a chance to work, develop new skills, and earn money.

These are some avenues that should not go unexplored in dealing with conduct-disordered adolescents. As I mentioned before, nobody can do it alone. The parent who tries can burn out rapidly.

Aside from professional help, which we will discuss in the next chapter, there are some readily accessible options that may help your troubled teen. These are by no means panaceas. And certainly I'm not suggesting that a boy who has been stealing and using drugs is going to experience a complete turnaround simply by joining the football team.

Sometimes, however, a team sport, a job, or a significant relationship with a respected person outside the inner circle of the immediate family can have a very positive impact on the conduct-disordered youth—especially when competent psychotherapy has laid the groundwork for change.

The earlier this positive influence appears, the better. But even under ideal conditions, you can't expect your child to accomplish an instant about-face. It will take time for him to integrate new habits and attitudes into his lifestyle.

THE HERO

Scott, an only child, had an alcoholic father and a mother who frequently turned up at local mental health clinics. From the time he was barely old enough to tie his shoes, Scott was pretty much on his own. His mother, depressed and withdrawn, spent most of the day in bed. When his father was home, he was usually more involved with his nightly fifth of whiskey than with his son.

A lonely little boy who grew into a withdrawn and sullen adolescent, Scott had little use for school. When he bothered to show up—which wasn't often—he was disruptive and argumentative. On most days, Scott could be found roaming the streets, looking as though he had no place to go. Once in a while he would go into a store and steal something. But mostly he stood and watched life going on around him, with the perspective of an outsider looking in.

When Scott was 14, something exciting happened. An uncle he had never met moved to their town. The uncle, a history professor at the local college, sensed Scott's unhappiness and took the boy under his wing. They began doing all the things that sons and fathers normally do—football games, movies, roughhousing, playing ball in the park. More importantly, Uncle Will became the boy's sounding board, someone Scott could talk to about everything that was happening in his life. He was also someone to admire, a role model for activities other than sitting around the house and drinking.

Eventually, Scott moved in with Uncle Will and under his tutelage decided to buckle down at school. The last time I heard from him he was in his freshman year at college.

This story had a happy ending. In Scott's case, his parents

allowed him to identify with a positive role model. True, it was mainly out of indifference that they were willing to let go. But the fact that they did forever changed their son's life.

Often, however, parents feel threatened by or even jealous of their child's relationship with an outsider. I've seen many cases where the parent, to meet his or her own emotional needs, actually interferes with the relationship.

Kids need to be allowed to choose their own heroes. And to be comfortable with their kids' choice, parents need to recognize their **own** insecurities and somehow resolve them.

It's worth noting that a good psychotherapist sometimes acts as this positive role model we're talking about. "Relationship therapy" encourages a kid who feels inadequate to identify with, and even borrow the skills of, the stronger, more competent therapist.

TALENT IN THE RAW

Laurette had an unhappy home life. Because her divorced mother had a long commute to her job and often had to work extra hours, Laurette had to spend Monday through Saturday of every week living with Mrs. Young, a paid caretaker. Mrs. Young kept Laurette clean, neat, and well-fed, but she didn't let her visit with friends or invite other kids over to the house. Lonely and depressed as a young child, Laurette rebelled when she reached her teens. She began to hang out with a drug-using crowd of kids who liked to party instead of going to school, and she became wild and promiscuous. Teachers mistrusted her, her grades sank rapidly, and she was on the verge of dropping out.

Then, in the fall of her sophomore year in high school, something unusual happened. To meet her gym requirement, Laurette chose dance, and found herself in the class of a woman teacher who actually seemed to like her. Mrs. Simon noticed that Laurette had excellent balance and a good sense of rhythm, and she praised her lavishly. Encouraged, Laurette started to make a point of being in school every day so she wouldn't miss dance. Then Mrs. Simon asked her to participate in a volunteer program where high school students tutored sixth-graders in modern dance. Helping the younger kids, Laurette felt needed and useful. She took a new pride in herself and in the rest of her schoolwork. When Mrs. Simon recommended her for a summer dance workshop at the end of the year, her self-esteem soared.

As a junior, Laurette became one of Mrs. Simon's proteges, studying advanced dance after school with a few other talented students. Gradually her reputation improved and she found herself among a new group of friends. She won a prize in a statewide dance competition, and was thrilled to see how much it meant to her mother. And in her senior year, with Mrs. Simon's advice and encouragement, Laurette applied to and was accepted by a professional dance school. Her whole life had turned around, thanks to a teacher who saw her potential and took an interest in her future. Laurette recently graduated and signed a contract with a dance company.

GET A JOB

A paid job can make a big difference in a kid's sense of independence and self-worth. Not that every youngster has a positive experience in the workplace. It's true that some kids act out on the job as much as they do at home or in school. They can't or won't do the work, and they end up getting fired.

Sometimes, though, a job is like a passport to a new world. We adults may not realize it, but many kids are anxious and insecure about job-hunting. If a teenager has low self-esteem, her fear of rejection may keep her from even trying to find work. Helping her find and succeed at her first paying job can boost her self-confidence enormously.

Barry grew up hearing how worthless he was. His parents were constantly harping on him to do his chores. Then when he finally did, they would give him "the look," sigh, and do the job over. His teachers had long ago given up on trying to teach him anything. And to the other kids, Barry was just "the dummy."

Then one summer the man next door asked Barry if he'd like a job helping him work in the yard. Reluctant at first, Barry decided the money was too good to pass up.

From the beginning it was clear that Barry was not only a hard worker, but also had a green thumb. Although he had never been a reader, he now began devouring gardening manuals, learning everything he could about various grass seeds and plants. The lawn that he seeded grew lush and green. He planted a vegetable garden and carved out flower beds, which he planted with an array of colorful annuals that mingled in perfect harmony.

At the end of that summer, Barry returned to school with a new wardrobe he had bought himself and, more important, a sense of confidence and accomplishment.

A job can serve several purposes. It can help identify a kid's strengths and weaknesses. For most, a job is the first place outside the home environment where a kid can experience himself in a straightforward and positive way. Paid employment can teach skills and bolster self-esteem, as the gardening work did for Barry.

Parents frequently make the mistake of minimizing their children's areas of interest and talent. We've all heard comments such as, "Playing the guitar isn't going to put food on the table, young man." A parent's put-down carries a cruel sting and tends to stifle a kid's creativity and spontaneity. No matter how insignificant and useless your child's interest strikes you, it's better to encourage and build on that interest than to ridicule it.

RELIGION

Many of the kids I see are hungry for something to believe in. Although I would never presume to promote any particular religion, I recognize that the depth and dignity of organized religious worship can have a positive effect on some youngsters. In fact, we have a pastor on our staff who not only conducts some of the group sessions, but also handles sex education. He's a great person to work with teenagers because he knows how to talk about important issues in a nonjudgmental way.

Since conflict over formal religious observance can arouse intense emotions within a family, many conduct-disordered kids tend to view religion as more of a problem than a solution.

Typically, I see this scenario. Janet's parents are fundamentalist Christians. They rarely miss a Sunday at church, and throughout the week they participate in many church-based social and charitable activities. Janet, however, doesn't see the point of going to church, and lately she's been balking. Churchgoing has turned into an issue of control.

Sometimes the way to get out of this trap is to negotiate a settlement: Janet will agree to go to church, but she gets to choose the church she wants to attend. This allows her to retain control and yet satisfies, to some degree anyway, her parents' wish that she respect a regular religious observance. If this type of settlement still doesn't meet a mother's and father's needs, they should seriously ask themselves why.

THE VALUE OF SPORTS

Sports are a wonderful experience for most kids. If I sound enthusiastic, it's because I am. Consider the advantages, and it becomes obvious why sports are usually a big plus factor in a kid's life. How many other activities allow you to bond with teammates, identify some of your strengths and weaknesses, and strive to imitate positive role models? Where is there a better chance to develop responsibility, work with a group, and feel the impact of your actions on the group's success or failure? If you're good enough, you may even end up getting an athletic scholarship for college!

Sports can also help keep a kid out of difficulties simply by occupying his time. "Jocks" who train seriously have less time to get in trouble than their peers who shun sports. Team sports, including baseball, football, basketball, and soccer, teach cooperation with others and instill respect for the rules and regulations of the game. This is excellent training for conduct-disordered youngsters who have problems dealing with authority. Challenging non-team sports, such as karate, weight-lifting, and dance, help a youngster develop a sense of self; they teach a great deal about the value of practice and perseverance.

Fine, you may say, but my son is a high school dropout who uses drugs and steals to pay for his habit. He's past the point where a significant role model or team membership can make a noticeable difference. Now what?

The final option is professional help in a hospital setting. Let's explore the treatment of conduct disorder in a structured inpatient program that's designed to help, not punish, troubled kids.

Chapter 10

When Professional Help Is Needed

I know a pediatrician who always asks parents certain questions during routine exams on children as young as 2 years old:

- Does she have any friends?
- Does she get invited more than once to a child's house to play?
- What does she do when someone pulls a toy away?
- Does she hug and kiss you?...

The list goes on and on. At first parents are a little puzzled by the doctor's questions. After all, they're there for a physical examination. But this physician explains to them that a child's social development is as important as her physical development.

I wish more primary care physicians were as developmentally oriented as this one.

Did you take your troubled adolescent to a pediatrician, only to have the doctor fill your ears with such platitudes as,

"Boys will be boys," or "She's just going through a rough adolescence"? At first you may have been reassured, since these words of wisdom were coming from a medical doctor. But something didn't ring true. Somehow chronic lying, stealing, and running away from home didn't strike you as a simple case of bumpy adolescence.

Unfortunately, the primary care physician—the man or woman on the front lines of health care—sometimes minimizes the seriousness of deviant behavior, giving it a falsely reassuring label such as "typical adolescent rebelliousness." This is actually a disservice to the parents, since it dissuades them from taking early action. The consequences of an overly nonchalant attitude can be serious.

Imagine what would happen if all doctors were like the developmentally oriented pediatrician. Think of the kids and families at risk who could be identified early, before destructive behavior patterns became entrenched. Think of the time they would save and the emotional upheaval they'd avoid! In many programs across the country, parents have been trained as therapists for their children. Moreover, they've been taught more effective parenting techniques. The results so far have been encouraging. As always, the keys are early identification of the problem and quick intervention.

As things now stand, it's typically not the pediatrician or family doctor, but rather someone associated with the child's school, who suspects a problem and encourages parents to let a mental health professional intervene. Usually this only happens after the small problems of childhood have exploded into the big problems of adolescence.

TREATMENT

By this time you know your son or daughter has a conduct disorder. Now the question is, what can you do about it? There are several components to treatment. Some kids with conduct disorder receive care on an outpatient basis, while others are hospitalized for a limited time. In our program, a combination of behavior modification techniques, psychotherapy, and family therapy is often used, in conjunction with our Escape to Reality physical challenge program. For many kids, medication play a role.

Let's look at some of these components of treatment.

THE USE OF MEDICATION

"No way, doctor. You're not giving my kid any of those drugs that turn people into zombies."

"Anything doctor. Try any drug, every drug, anything you think will make her well."

These are the polar opposites of parent attitudes toward the use of psychoactive medication in the treatment of conduct disorder. First, let me stress that not every kid with conduct disorder is a candidate for medication. The prime determinant is whether the youngster's objectionable behavior seems to have a biological basis. For example, if the kid is showing signs of attention deficit disorder, I may try a medication that may calm his intensely fidgety behavior and lengthen his attention span. On the other hand, if the unacceptable behavior seems to be a simple function of the adolescent's mishandling of life's difficulties, or of an anxiety disorder, drugs may not be very effective or different medications may have to be considered.

I try medication in about 50 percent of the kids I see. As noted before, medicine seems to make a remarkable difference in about 25 percent of these cases, a modest difference in another 25 to 50 percent, and no perceptible difference in the final 25 percent.

Here are some of the drugs we use, often in combinations:

Psychostimultants: These medications are tried when there's a suspected diagnosis of attention deficit disorder, with or without hyperactivity. Ritalin, Dexedrine, and Cylert are common psychostimulants. While it may seem strange to prescribe a stimulant for a kid who is climbing the walls from excess energy, these drugs can have a paradoxical calming effect that enables a child with ADD to concentrate better.

Potential side effects include disturbed sleep, loss of appetite, headache, stomachache, rapid heartbeat, changes in blood pressure, and dizziness. A potential long-term side effect is a slowing of weight gain or growth.

Ritalin in particular has received bad press, which may be partly deserved. Although Ritalin is an excellent medication when used appropriately, some less-than-responsible clinicians tend to prescribe it far too readily for any child reported to be a discipline problem. Beware of the shotgun approach to behavior difficulties.

Antidepressants: Medications such as Elavil, Norpramin, and Tofranil—or the next generation of antidepressants such as Prozac—may be used if depression is suspected. They are sometimes used in conjunction with other psychotropic medications, such as lithium, to treat an assortment of mood disorders or anxiety-related issues.

A great deal of research has been done on the use of antidepressants with conduct-disordered kids. It's been found that certain subgroups of conduct problems tend to respond to particular medications. Side effects of antidepressants may include blurry vision, dry mouth, sleepiness, constipation, or rapid pulse.

Lithium: Lithium carbonate is a mood stabilizer that may be used in combination with an antidepressant. This natural mineral salt can sometimes smooth out the extreme highs and lows that characterize manic-depressive disorders.

Side effects include sleepiness, confusion, tremor, headache, diarrhea, restlessness, rashes, and hallucinations.

Antiseizure Medications: Tegretol, the antiseizure medication we most often use, is the drug of choice for the control of a wide range of seizures. In may also help kids who have episodic violent outbursts, or atypical mood disturbances that include irritable, impulsive, volatile behavior.

In some studies, Tegretol has proved a safe alternative to

lithium for the treatment of manic-depressive disorder. At other times it works well in tandem with other psychotropic medications. It may also be effective in the treatment of depression. Possible side effects include drowsiness, irritability, and an interference with normal blood cell formation that requires close monitoring.

In evaluating whether or not a kid should have medication, parents must understand what the drug may or may not do. It's best to avoid unrealistic expectations. Ritalin may enable Jim to sit still and concentrate for the first time in his life, but it won't magically erase his fifteen years of academic failure and the resultant erosion of his self-esteem. Jim will need other forms of therapy to build up his sense of himself as a worthwhile person.

Few parents understand intuitively what it means to a kid to be put on psychiatric medication. To a youngster, having to take medicine means being sick—a "nut case." This is why many teenagers resist medication, insisting they're all right, they don't need that stuff.

My philosophy is never to put a kid on medication out of the blue. Starting medication requires a lot of discussion. It has to be integrated gently into the kid's life, and understood from a developmental perspective. Adolescents in general tend to be somewhat grandiose and to see themselves as invulnerable. Having to take medication pricks that bubble of invulnerability, and thus poses problems for many kids.

"Will I need to take these pills for the rest of my life?" Every kid who begins treatment with medication wants to know when it will end. There's no way to know. My usual approach is to say, "Let's give it a try and see what happens." If a kid responds well to the medication, I continue it for a while, then take him off to see how well he does.

Once their behavior stabilizes, many kids do just fine without any further medication. A few don't. Those who are helped by lithium, for example, often need to take the drug for a number of years.

Like all medications, psychoactive drugs should be taken seriously. I can't overemphasize the importance of frequent careful monitoring by a board-certified psychiatrist who is trained in their use. After a kid leaves the hospital, she should be referred to a psychiatrist who will see her on a regular basis, monitor her medication dosage, and work with her in deciding how to proceed.

"ON THE COUCH"

If you mention psychotherapy to most people, the image that comes to mind is a bearded, bespectacled doctor in a three-piece suit. Puffing on his pipe, the good Herr Doktor invites the patient to recline on his leather couch and talk about his past.

Psychotherapy can be that. But it can also be much more. Simply stated, psychotherapy is the treatment of psychological problems. Therefore, anything that deals with those problems is psychotherapy. Finding a kid a volunteer job, giving him effective medication, or helping him relate to kids in a group session are all valid forms of psychotherapy— different from the session on the couch, but just as important.

I'm not knocking traditional on-the-couch psychiatry. In fact, I'm a proponent of analytical psychotherapy, and I incorporate its principles in our individual, group, and family therapy approaches at the hospital. But for conduct-disordered kids, pure analysis isn't the treatment of choice. You can't usually expect to sit right down and have a cogent, rational discussion of feelings with a kid who's used to arguing, fighting, lying, stealing, skipping school, and running away from home. Until that behavior starts to change, classic analysis doesn't stand much of a chance.

Also, many kids with conduct disorder talk a good line. They typically shy away from delving too deeply into their feelings, and they may try to con a therapist into thinking he has broken through the barrier. Mentally as sharp as knives, these kids could sell snow to the Eskimos.

The traditional image of the psychiatrist is one of aloofness and impartiality. I think one of the secrets of our program's success is that I don't allow the professionals—the "grownups" —to stand on the sidelines. Personally, I like to mix it up with these kids. This seems to be the only way to get to them—someone needs to create the bond. In essence, I establish a personal relationship with each and every one. This is particularly important since most of the kids I see have had disturbed relationships with adults in the past. They haven't "bought in" to the idea that a teenager and an adult can relate to each other openly and honestly. To me and to them, it's a moving experience to reach a point where we can communicate directly on an emotional level.

SHARP AND ABRASIVE

I'm not saying these are easy youngsters to deal with. Most psychiatrists fear conduct-disordered kids and prefer not to treat them. But I genuinely like these kids. They're constantly pushing, trying to drive me over the edge, and something in me responds to that challenge. They can spot my weaknesses and zero in on them with laser-like intensity— and even though that's annoying, it's also intriguing.

A recent example comes to mind. The kids in the program decided I wore my pants too short. One day I walked into a group session and they all had their pants rolled up to their knees. I can't pretend that they didn't strike a sensitive nerve. But it was also funny, and in the end I couldn't help laughing at their joke. It eventually led to a discussion on people's sensitivity, self-esteem, and self-image.

One patient who deliberately tried to be hurtful was Kurt, a pale, emaciated boy with a severe case of acne. Kurt affected a neo-Nazi ideology, always dressed in full battle regalia, and seemed totally incapable of relating to people in a relaxed, friendly way. Whenever he saw me he would click his heels, salute "Heil Hitler," and say things like, "I'm going to put your mother in the ovens." I didn't react, just listened.

Part of our program here at the hospital is Escape to Reality, a specially designed physical obstacle course that promotes trust through cooperation in overcoming challenges. Climbing a sheer thirty-foot wall while someone belays you (holds your safety rope) is one of the exercises that demands a high degree of confidence. One day Kurt admitted that he wasn't confident belaying anyone who was climbing the wall. From a psychological standpoint this seemed highly significant. According to my interpretation, Kurt was saying he felt like a lightweight, a person no one could depend on.

I told Kurt I would trust him to belay me as I inched my way to the dizzying 30-foot height—and that's what we did. It was a highly emotional experience. I admit I had moments of considerable anxiety! But he held the rope tight and all went well.

Afterward, Kurt had a new confidence in himself. I noticed that he suddenly began to relate more naturally both to me and to the other kids. No, this single event didn't turn him into a college-bound yuppie with Wall Street aspirations. But no one could deny that his behavior and his ability to relate had taken a remarkable turn for the better.

MIXING IT UP

For treatment to be effective, it's critical that the program director be more than just an authority figure, a naysayer. You can't run this show the way Judge Wapner runs *People's Court*. It's useless to try to intimidate the kids into acceptable behavior. Rules, of course, are necessary and important—they form one piece of the puzzle. But stringent rules alone won't make much of a dent in the treatment of conduct disorder.

It's important for our kids to have input into the major decisions that affect their lives. Every day we have a meeting of the entire staff-and-patient community, and it's the kids who run the show. They have a president and a governing body, similar to a school student council. This is the forum where they're allowed and, in fact, encouraged to air their complaints—the rooms are too hot or too cold, someone wants a change of roommate, a new kid is breaking rules, and so on. It's a real treat to see kids who have typically been outcasts gradually assuming positions of leadership, and making decisions on ethical grounds. They take their patient-government responsibility very seriously, which shows how much it touches their self-image. One of their most impressive responsibilities is deciding if someone should be temporarily removed from the community because of unacceptable behavior.

THE CONDUCT DISORDER PROGRAM AT LAUREL OAKS HOSPITAL

Here are some of the most commonly asked questions regarding our program for conduct disordered adolescents at Laurel Oaks Hospital in Orlando, Florida:

What are the accommodations like?

Currently, we have space for twenty-four kids. Each teen shares a room with someone of the same sex, with two rooms sharing a bathroom. Boys are housed in one part of the unit and girls in another.

What about school?

There is a school in the hospital. A certified teacher conducts classes every weekday. All patients must attend class.

Is treatment the same for every child?

Definitely not. On the first day the youngster is evaluated by a psychiatric nurse or social worker, who recommends either an inpatient or outpatient treatment program. When hospitalization is advised, I meet with the kid to get a brief history and to do a mental status exam (a series of tests to determine if she is thinking clearly). Based on our meeting, I recommend a battery of psychological and sometimes neurological tests.

During the first two weeks of hospitalization there may be other evaluations, such as hormone tests that may suggest the presence of a mood disorder.

The teenager is assigned a psychotherapist with whom she will meet individually twice a week. An important point is that the psychotherapist has nothing to do with discipline on the unit. He serves as the adolescent's advocate but has no administrative power. A kid has no reason to sweet-talk her therapist, because she can't get anything from him. I am the disciplinarian for the unit. In that role, I try to stay objective and neutral.

In the initial days of your teenager's hospitalization, the staff gets together to construct a treatment plan that's based on the results of the tests, interviews with the family, and discussions with the child herself. Depending upon the findings, treatment may include medication, one-on-one psychotherapy, group therapy, family counseling, Escape to Reality training, and a volunteer job.

What is the length of hospitalization?

Most kids are in the hospital between thirty and sixty days.

Will my child be "well" when he comes home?

Aftercare is a critical part of our program and one that we begin addressing from the onset of treatment. Who will supervise medications, if any are recommended? What kind of family environment will the kid go home to? Will the school be supportive to his needs? Would a job help?

An important factor in the success of treatment is the home environment to which the adolescent returns. When the family atmosphere is positive, many kids continue to do well after they go home. When it is negative, a kid who has done extremely well in the hospital and has left with a positive attitude may quickly relapse into his old self-defeating way.

If his family is unable to provide the necessary structure and support, it may be desirable for the teenager to go directly from the hospital to a group home or some similar setting that offers a stable and supportive environment. Since group homes for adolescents are few and far between, this is a viable alternative for only a limited number of youngsters.

EPILOGUE

A Beginning

A few days ago I bumped into Barbara at the supermarket where she has a part-time job bagging groceries. Six months ago she was spaced out on drugs, sleeping on any empty mattress she could find, and spending her days in crack houses. At 16, she was withering. She didn't have much incentive to make it to 17.

It was hard to imagine that this girl with the quick smile, sparkling eyes, and glowing skin was the same person who had opened her wrists with a razor blade a few months before.

"I don't need your help," she had screamed at me the day her parents brought her to the hospital. "You can't make me change."

Barbara, like many kids who come to our program, was initially determined to go it alone. But at some point during her two-month hospitalization, something fell into place for her.

"No, things aren't perfect," she told me at the grocery store. She still gets depressed sometimes, and the urge to get back on drugs can be powerful. But so far she has managed to take control of her life and steer it in the only direction that offers hope. She's back in school, with a lot of catching up to do, but she's taking it one day at a time. The job at the supermarket has made her feel she can do something useful. And her relationship with her parents—while still far from perfect—is improving with the help of weekly therapy sessions.

For the first time in her life, Barbara dares to feel hopeful about her future.

Hope—that's what I want you to take away with you after reading this book.

When a kid makes a career of getting in trouble, it's easy to cast blame: "It's his fault." "It's their fault." "It's your fault." In reality, it's probably a little bit of everybody's fault.

The past, of course, is beyond our control. The only point in delving into it is to understand what happened and why it should not be repeated. You may want to recognize and acknowledge any mistakes you've made in parenting your child. But you can't allow guilt to keep you from setting a new course for the future.

No, it won't be easy. As you may have gathered by now, the treatment of conduct disorder follows a steep and winding path. Getting all the way to the top requires commitment from both the adolescent and the family.

There are no written guarantees.

But there is hope. And hope, combined with a good treatment plan and the determination to follow it, is surely the most powerful of medicines.

Sources

Aichhorn, August. *Wayward Youth*. New York: Viking, 1951.

Behrman, Richard E. and Vaughan III, Victor C., eds. *Nelson's Textbook of Pediatrics* (13th edition). Philadelphia: Saunders, 1987.

Berkovitz, Irving. "Aggression, Adolescence, and Schools." *Adolescent Psychiatry*, vol. 14, 483-99, 1987.

Chagoya, Leopoldo and Schkolne, Theo. "Children Who Lie: A Review of the Literature." *Canadian Journal of Psychiatry*, vol. 31, no. 7, 665-69, 1986.

Chamberlain, P. and Patterson G. R. "Aggressive Behavior in Middle Childhood." Chapter in *The Clinical Guide to Child Psychiatry*. Edited by D. Shaffer, et al. New York: The Free Press, 1985.

Goldstein, Harris S. "Parental Composition, Supervision, and Conduct Problems in Youths 12 to 17 Years Old." *Journal of the American Academy of Child Psychiatry*, vol. 23, no. 6, 679-84, 1984.

Gorky, Maxim. *My Childhood*. Translated by Ronald Wilks. Middlesex, England: Penguin Books Ltd., 1966.

Greenhill, Laurence L., "Pediatric Psychopharmacology." Chapter in *The Clinical Guide to Child Psychiatry*. Edited by D. Shaffer, et al. New York: The Free Press, 1985.

Ingersoll, Barbara. *Your Hyperactive Child: A Parents Guide to Coping with Attention Deficit Disorder*. New York: Doubleday, 1988.

Kay, Rena L., and Kay, Jerald. "Adolescent Conduct Disorders." Chapter 22 in the American Psychiatric Association's *Annual Review of Psychiatry - Volume 5*. Edited by Allen J. Frances and Robert E. Hales. Washington: American Psychiatric Press, 1986.

Kelso, Jane and Stewart, Mark A. "Factors Which Predict the Persistence of Aggressive Conduct Disorder." *Journal of Child Psychology and Psychiatry*, vol. 27, no. 1, 77-86, 1986.

Lahey, Benjamin B., et al. "Psychopathology in the Parents of Children with Conduct Disorder and Hyperactivity." *Journal of the American Academy of Child and Adolescent Psychiatry*, vol. 27, no. 2, 163-70, 1988.

Lewis, D.O., "Juvenile Delinquency." Chapter in *The Clinical Guide to Child Psychiatry*. Edited by D. Shaffer, et al. New York: The Free Press, 1985.

Magid, Ken and Mckelvey, Carol. *High Risk: Children Without a Conscience*. Golden, Colorado: M & M Publishing, 1987.

Meeks, John E. *High Times/Low Times: The Many Faces of Adolescent Depression*. Summit, NJ: PIA Press, 1988.

Offer, Daniel. "Adolescent Development: A Normative Perspective." Chapter 18 in the American Psychiatric Association's *Annual Review of Psychiatry - Volume 5*. Edited by Allen J. Frances and Robert E. Hales. Washington: American Psychiatric Press, 1986.

Webster-Stratton, Carolyn. "Comparison of Abusive and Nonabusive Families with Conduct-Disordered Children." *American Journal of Orthopsychiatry*, vol. 55, no. 1, 59-69, 1985.

Webster-Stratton, Carolyn. "Intervention Approaches to Conduct Disorders in Young Children." *Nurse Practitioner*, May 1983, 23-34.

Webster-Stratton, Carolyn. "Randomized Trial of Two Parent-Training Programs for Families with Conduct-Disordered Children." *Journal of Consulting and Clinical Psychology*, vol. 52, no. 4, 666-78, August, 1984.

Weisberg, Lynne, and Greenberg, Rosalie. *When Acting Out Isn't Acting*. Summit, NJ: PIA Press, 1988.

Index

ABOUT THE AUTHOR

Alan M. Cohen, M.D. is the Medical Director of Laurel Oaks Hospital in Orlando, Florida. The youngest of PIA's Medical Directors, Dr. Cohen was recently named their "Medical Director of the Year." This was due in part to the extensive research he has conducted in the field of adolescent conduct disorders. At Laurel Oaks, he also serves as Clinical Director for their "Operation Redirect" program, a highly specialized program that deals with acting-out adolescents.

In addition, Dr. Cohen hosts a daily radio program that focuses on children's issues. Considered Central Florida's expert, he has been asked to speak on all of the local TV stations, and to various community groups.